THE OFFICIAL SCRIPT BOOK

THE OFFICIAL SCRIPT BOOK

SCREENPLAY BY

Matt Reeves & Peter Craig

BATMAN CREATED BY

Bob Kane with Bill Finger

INSIGHT
EDITIONS

San Rafael • Los Angeles • London

A CONVERSATION WITH
MATT REEVES

JANUARY 12, 2022

QUESTION: What is it about this character that you love that inspired your take on this script, because it's uncharted territory on the screen?

MATT REEVES: You know, I think the thing that most affected me about his character, and I've loved the character since I was a kid, I mean, since Adam West... Batman obviously is incredibly cool. There's something about this character in the midst of all this kind of corruption who decides to don a suit and has all of these amazing gadgets and goes out and does all this stuff that as a kid, I found incredibly captivating, as you would, and as the world does. But I think that as a filmmaker, what was exciting to me in having a chance to approach the character is that as a comic book character, or a superhero character, he's not a superhero. He is a character who's trying to make meaning out of his life. He's never gotten over what happened to him as a kid.

And so, he's trying to make sense of it by throwing himself headlong into a completely dangerous situation. And he's not in control of himself. At least that's my vision for it. And that's what I wanted this iteration to be. I felt like there'd been a lot of great origin tales that had been done in the movies. And you'd seen Bruce lose his parents and then struggle and decide to try and perfect himself to become a vigilante. And I didn't want to do that because I felt it had already been done well more than once. But what I thought I hadn't seen was a version where the arc is actually Batman's arc—where you meet him and he's already Batman, but there's such a distance to travel in terms of what he's going to become and what he is that there's a lot that needs to be awakened in him for him to become better.

QUESTION: So how would you describe the Batman we meet in this film?

MATT REEVES: You see a guy who is sort of almost like a vision of horror; he comes to the shadows and he's meant to intimidate the criminal element. But the real question is, what happens to you when you put on a mask and you have that anonymity? You kind of lose yourself. This is a guy who is not only fighting the criminal element, he's fighting himself. And he doesn't even know he's fighting himself. Because all of this is driven by the fact that he has never gotten over the trauma from his childhood. I think what excited me was this notion that he would be a character with so many layers, that he would be a superhero whose only real superpower is his will to push himself to extreme lengths in order to try to find a way to make meaning and to help people in the city. Not because he's doing it out of the goodness of his heart, but because it's the only way he can find meaning in such a difficult world.

QUESTION: And he also has a mystery to solve, correct?

MATT REEVES: Yes, I think that's really it. I mean, I think this is the other thing that I really felt hadn't been done was leaning into that character as a detective, as the world's greatest detective. This all began with Bob Kane and Bill Finger as a pure noir story; it was a reaction to Superman, and the idea of that kind of tremendous optimism, the American-dream optimism of that. It was the flip side of it and the idea of a really corrupt world and somebody at the center of it as the person who could be a champion to fight against the corruption. I think that was based very much in

that kind of noir idea of the detective. And he was supposed to be the world's greatest, and I don't think any of the movies, while they've touched on the idea that he is, they've never made that the subject of the movie. And I just felt like, to tell a story in which this vigilante is also learning to be an incredible detective, putting the pieces together and trying to solve the mysteries of why this city is so corrupt... I didn't think we'd seen that before. And so that was the other thing that I felt would be really definitive in this and that it would enable us to get into the corruption and history of a place, and that place is Gotham.

So, they're all the things that are iconic Batman, but had never been quite done that way in the movies. And I think that there was no way to approach this character again without feeling like we were doing it in a different way, because there have been great Batman movies and the only way to try and do something else is to try and be different.

QUESTION: While you've created your own space with this story, there's clearly a nod or two to some of the really iconic comics, like *Year One*, *The Long Halloween*, and so many other things. So I think you're serving the fans in a way they may not even be expecting.

MATT REEVES: Well, that was actually the goal. One of the first things I did when I sat down to do this was I went on a deep dive with the comics and I just started reading them all.

As I said, my big entry into being a Batman fan was Batman '66 and Adam West, and Neal Adams, and obviously the earlier comics. But I did a dive on everything that had been done since then, because I hadn't read it all. And here's what's crazy when you mentioned *The Long Halloween*. My screenwriting teacher, the person who told me at USC that I should become a writer, was Jeph Loeb.

QUESTION: Who wrote *The Long Halloween*, of course!

MATT REEVES: And he wrote that and many others after he was my teacher. But he wrote some of the most definitive, modern-day Batman stories and I hadn't actually read them. And so when I read them, I knew that I wanted to do a noir and I knew I wanted to do a story about a serial killer that was The Riddler. And then when I read *The Long Halloween*, I was like, "Oh my God, this is so inspirational." And so it really was absolutely an attempt to find the things that I connected to in the comics. So, it wasn't something where it was like, "Oh, let me just find a way to put the comics in here." It was me going on a deep dive to find those things that resonated with me. And the ones that you mentioned, I really connected to very strongly. I connected to *The Long Halloween*. I connected in a major way to *Year One*. I connected to Darwyn Cooke's *Ego*. All the things that got into tone and psychology and the way of telling a certain story. And so then when you absorb all of that, it can't help but filter into the storytelling. And so, yeah, I do hope that true fans of the comics are going to find, in ways they never expected, hopefully, things that connect to the comics that they love.

QUESTION: Tell me about Rob Pattinson, because, by the way, just his jawline and profile are pretty perfect, as I think everyone who's ever drawn Batman would agree.

MATT REEVES: Everyone has drawn a Pattinson-like jawline.

QUESTION: Exactly! So, tell me about working with him.

MATT REEVES: It was fabulous. I mean, the thing about it is, as I was writing, I started trying to look at actors in the age range that I was thinking of for the character, once it became clear that I could do a younger Batman. And I wanted this Batman to be someone who was in conflict with himself, somebody who had a sense of danger, somebody who had a kind of sexiness to him, somebody who looked like he was desperate, someone who could show vulnerability because I felt like Batman was all those things. And I wanted an actor with whom you could feel all those things very palpably. Almost like a young Brando or Montgomery Clift, where you could feel that sort of almost method energy, right?

QUESTION: Yes!

MATT REEVES: And when I started watching all these Rob movies, and when I saw him in *Good Time*, I was like, it has to be this guy—without knowing whether or not he would ever...because all he's done after the *Twilight* movies is gone out and been in all of these really interesting indie movies. So, I had no idea whether or not he would ever be interested in doing a big comic book character franchise. I just had no idea. But it didn't matter. I wrote it for him. And then it turned out, and I actually said to Dylan, my partner Dylan Clark, I said, "What if Rob doesn't want to do this? That's going to be a real bummer. I really see him." And then he told me that he had this meeting with him, he said, "You know, he asked me about it," and I was like, "Really?" He said, "Yeah, I think he likes Batman." And a long time after that, when I finally finished the script—because I'm not fast [LAUGHS]—we met and we really connected over it.

QUESTION: What was his initial reaction?

MATT REEVES: And you know, what I love about Rob is he never wants to go at something the straight-on way. And he's looking for the ways in which somebody is off and different and weird and struggling. And those are all the things that I find interesting; we really connected on that. I think he understood that this guy was doing things in a way that really, on one level, made no sense and that he was a kind of freak of sorts. And I think he related to those things and it's something I think that draws him to the characters that he chooses. I was working with him and trying to find the way to

realize this new character, and to try and find a way to get
Rob's performance to come through. I think this is the most
challenging Batman in the sense that there are a lot of the
most emotional scenes, and then he has a real muscularity as
Batman. I wanted him to have a kind of fierceness and
volatility and a kind of dangerousness, but I also needed him
actually to be desperate and emotional. And all of these
things that he had to somehow project through the cowl,
that's not easy. We worked a lot on that and we worked on
"what does his voice sound like?" And in all of these things
Rob is very instinctual, and it was a really great experience. It
was really fun to do, we were always exploring... I think we

both loved the character, but we loved the idea also of doing him in a different way. And we were just constantly pushing ourselves to do that.

QUESTION: Zoë Kravitz—you also are reinventing Catwoman, Selina Kyle, bringing her to life in a way we've never seen before.

MATT REEVES: One of the things that I wanted to do was that, because it wasn't Batman's origin tale, but it was his early days, I wanted him to be pursuing the clues of the case and have it touch on some of the iconic Batman Rogues Gallery characters. And in their case as well it would be their origins. In many of the comics, Batman making an appearance in Gotham City is what inspired Catwoman to become Catwoman. She thinks, "Oh, this guy's wearing the suit. What is that? What an interesting idea." And so he's having an effect on the city he never meant to have, which is that he's actually inspiring some of the criminals and some of the Rogues Gallery characters to adopt these kinds of alter egos. And in the case of Selina Kyle, I wanted him to meet her along the way. Let's say the way that Jake Gittes met Evelyn Mulwray in *Chinatown*, where she's involved in a case and he's very suspicious of her. And he automatically assumes, because he's very cynical about this place, that because of the world and the people she's involved in, that she must have questionable morals.

Selina Kyle has always been a very compelling character because she didn't have the resources that Bruce Wayne did. She had to grow up in a very tough place and find a way to survive. And who is he to judge when she didn't have the things that he had and he doesn't really know who she is?

I really needed to find somebody who could embody this
character, not so much in a kind of theatrical style, because
obviously I think Michelle Pfeiffer is the best example of that;
she was incredible as Catwoman. The Burton film was so
theatrical, and it was stunning. I'll never forget it; I just think
she was incredible, she just popped off of the screen and was
larger than life. But I wanted this version to be rooted in the
Selina Kyle side of the character, more so than Catwoman,
because she isn't exactly Catwoman yet. So I needed
somebody to really give her a kind of specificity and life and
soul. Zoë came in and read for the role and she just got it. I
mean, I think she's incredible. And she just had such a

thoughtful understanding of the character and really wanted to find a way to make her flesh and blood. And that's what we tried to do, so that it's a version of the character that I think is as human as Bruce Wayne.

Zoë really imbued her with a real kind of fight and struggle that comes from where she comes from. You look at her and you say, "That's where Selina Kyle came from." She had to fight tooth and nail. There's a lot of Easter eggs that connect to the comics in that, too, and I think that'll be fun for the fans. And Zoë was a big part of that, she read the comics and there were certain images she wanted. She came in and she said she

had this idea about wanting to recreate one of the *Year One* images, and I was like, "Totally!" She had a lot of really fun ideas that we just leaned into together. She was hugely influential in terms of determining the character and it was really great to work with her.

QUESTION: I would love to talk about every single element of the film with you, but we'll leave it here for audiences to be surprised when they see the film. Thank you so much for your time.

MATT REEVES: My pleasure.

THE BATMAN
THE SHOOTING SCRIPT

written by
Matt Reeves & Peter Craig

BLACK SCREEN

The quiet hum of CITY TRAFFIC and DISTANT SIRENS. Gradually, we make out something unnerving, right beside us: **SOMEONE BREATHING...** A MASSIVE RED TITLE FADES UP:

"THE BATMAN"

HOLD; then SMASH OUT OF THE BLACKNESS TO REVEAL—

AN OUT OF FOCUS BINOCULAR POV—DUSK

We FOCUS, SEARCHING THE FACADE OF AN OPULENT TOWNHOUSE... The **BREATHING SUDDENLY QUIETS** as a SHAPE APPEARS IN A WINDOW—a LITTLE RED NINJA gazes out, clutching a small sword. The ninja spins, brandishing the sword as TWO SHAPES enter behind him—a WOMAN, late 30s, dressed as a WITCH—and a MAN, late 50s, in a WELL-CUT SUIT.

The little ninja rushes in, "stabbing" the Man, who collapses melodramatically. The Woman smiles—speaks to the ninja, and he grabs a PUMPKIN CANDY BUCKET as they start to exit. The Man sits up, yells after them; the ninja runs back for a hug. Finally, the ninja and Woman exit, LEAVING THE MAN ALONE. He grows SOBER. As the Man pulls himself up, the **BREATHING BESIDE US RESUMES**...

INT. OPULENT TOWNHOUSE—DIMLY-LIGHTED STUDY—NIGHT

In the light of the flickering TV, we see now the Man is handsome, distinguished. He stands, sipping scotch, watching THE NEWS; a CHYRON reads, "GOTHAM MAYORAL RACE":

> FEMALE NEWSCASTER (ON TV)
> Just-released polls have incumbent mayor, Don Mitchell, Jr. and twenty-eight-year-old grassroots challenger, Bella Reál in a dead heat. Things certainly got hot last night in their final debate before next Tuesday's election...

As the Man anxiously watches the DEBATE CLIP, we realize: he is MAYOR MITCHELL; his female challenger, BELLA REÁL, young, intelligent, a force of nature, shares the stage—

> MAYOR MITCHELL (ON TV)
> Now my young opponent here wants to gut the Gotham Renewal Program established by the great Thomas Wayne, cutting the funds for vital projects like our sea wall, and the safety net for those in need—

BELLA REÁL (ON TV)
—the Renewal Program is broken! The city's been "renewing" for twenty years, look where it's gotten us! Crime has skyrocketed!

MAYOR MITCHELL (ON TV)
Now wait a minute—hold on—!

BELLA REÁL (ON TV)
Murder and drug use are at historic highs! We have a masked vigilante running the streets!

MAYOR MITCHELL (ON TV)
—under my administration the Gotham PD dealt major blows against organized crime and drug trafficking! The Salvatore Maroni case was the biggest drug bust in city history—

BELLA REÁL (ON TV)
—but drops and other drugs are still rampant! It's gotten worse!

MAYOR MITCHELL (ON TV)
I'm not saying there isn't work to do—but listen—I have a beautiful wife and young son, OK? I will not rest until this city is safe for them—and all our citizens!

Mitchell turns, startled, as a PHONE RINGS. As he EXITS FRAME to answer, we STAY on a DARK HALL BEHIND THE STUDY—on the wall by the doorway, we see a framed headline: "**MARONI DRUG BUST! MAYOR'S STING OPERATION HISTORIC**".

As the TV brightens, we SEE for the first time, SOMEONE IS IN THE HALL. Barely visible, the Figure wears a DARK, OLIVE GREEN HOOD— a homemade executioner's mask, with PRESCRIPTION AVIATOR GLASSES bizarrely outside the hood.

> MAYOR MITCHELL (OS)
> Hey. Yeah, I'm watching GC1...

As Mitchell PACES IN AND OUT OF FRAME, the Figure's hooded head ominously tracks him...

> MAYOR MITCHELL (OS)
> Why is she still <u>tied</u>—I thought
> we were getting a <u>bump</u> in the
> new Post poll...? OK, you know
> what? I can't, I can't watch this
> anymore—call me in the
> morning—

We HEAR the phone hang up, and Mitchell RE-ENTERS FRAME, agitated; as he SHUTS OFF THE TV, the HALL BEHIND HIM SUDDENLY GOES DARK, the **FIGURE NO LONGER IN SIGHT**.

Mitchell stands there, drink in hand; starts to sip, as—**THE FIGURE LURCHES OUT OF THE DARK**—**FRANTICALLY CLUBBING HIM OVER AND OVER**—suddenly, the **WEAPON SLIPS LOOSE**—it **SKITTERS** right at us and **STOPS**. **A GLEAMING METAL TOOL**. Whatever it is, it's

WET with blood. The Figure turns, <u>PANTING</u>, rises off the motionless victim, trudges over to us... <u>A GLOVED HAND retrieves the strange weapon</u>.

The Figure walks back, regarding the victim for a long, creepy moment... then stretches its arms as far as they will go, <u>LOUDLY UNSPOOLING a LONG PIECE OF SILVER DUCT TAPE</u>... And with a LOW RUMBLE OF THUNDER, we SLAM INTO—

BLACKNESS AGAIN...

We HEAR PATTERING RAIN as a HYPNOTIC VOICE OVER begins:

VOICE OVER
Thursday, October thirty-first...

A GAS ARC BULB BURNS to life... glowing BRIGHTER...
BRIGHTER... REVEALING: <u>We're INSIDE A SEARCHLIGHT</u>...

EXT. ROOFTOP—ON THE RUSTED SEARCHLIGHT—NIGHT

As the LIGHT INTENSIFIES—RAINDROPS ILLUMINATE—
BEATING and DANCING CHAOTICALLY on the hot lens—

EXT. RAINY GOTHAM STREETS—HIGH ANGLE—NIGHT

A bacchanalian Times Square vibe. **COSTUMED
HALLOWEEN REVELERS** swarm wet sidewalks in the glow
of NEON and LED.

> VOICE OVER
> The city streets are crowded for
> the holiday, even with the rain...

MOVING POV—ON THE SIDEWALK

We PUSH INTO the sea of COSPLAYERS, CLUBBERS,
TOURISTS...

> VOICE OVER
> Hidden in the chaos... is the
> <u>element</u>. Waiting to strike like
> <u>snakes</u> at the decent... the
> vulnerable...

A MALE FIGURE suddenly ENTERS FRAME—

> VOICE OVER
> But <u>I'm</u> there too, <u>watching</u>...

FOLLOW FROM BEHIND as he WALKS in ARMY JACKET, KNIT CAP, a DUFFEL on his shoulder. He looks like a **DRIFTER...**

<u>SUPER-TIGHT ON THE **DRIFTER'S INTENSE EYES** AS HE WALKS...</u>

> VOICE OVER
> Two years of nights have turned
> me into a nocturnal animal... My
> senses are heightened now... I
> can almost <u>smell</u> them...

EXT. BODEGA—MOVING POV TOWARD THE WINDOW—NIGHT

PEER IN at the few COSTUMED SHOPPERS inside; a GUY in a HOODIE and YELLOW SAD EMOJI MASK steps to the counter—

> VOICE OVER
> I must choose my targets
> carefully...

INSIDE

<u>Sad Emoji NERVOUSLY PULLS A GUN on the CASHIER!</u>

> SAD EMOJI
> C'mon...!

EXT. COLOSSAL GOTHAM BANK—MOVING POV—NIGHT

We SPY THREE VANDALS, SPRAY-PAINTING the huge pillars—

> VOICE OVER
> It's a big city, I can't be
> everywhere...

THE VANDALS wear GUY FAWKES MASKS—one LIGHTS A MOLOTOV COCKTAIL—HURLS IT, SHATTERING THE GLASS FRONT DOOR—

INT. A SPEEDING ELEVATED TRAIN—LURKING POV—NIGHT

WE PEER THROUGH the CONNECTING DOOR INTO THE CAR AHEAD—where EIGHT GANG MEMBERS in SKULL FACE PAINT carouse—

> VOICE OVER
> But they don't know where I
> am...

THE CAR AHEAD

The gang crowds, jockeying to see a CELLPHONE VIDEO.

TIGHT ON THE VIDEO

THE GANG striding through a park—ONE points at a RANDOM JOGGER—ANOTHER responds, PUNCHING HIM OUT!

THE GANG WATCHING THE CELLPHONE

recoils with LAUGHTER—when THE GANG LEADER notices a LONE PASSENGER rising as the TRAIN SLOWS. He turns to a YOUNGER MEMBER, nodding toward the Passenger with a menacing smile—as the Young Member looks anxiously—

EXT. A SHADOWY SPACE—NIGHT

FINGERS QUICKLY SMEAR BLACK CAMO PAINT around fierce eyes, veiled in darkness—as we spot THE DRIFTER'S ARMY DUFFLE on wet ground—inside, we GLIMPSE **THE BAT COWL**!

EXT. ROOFTOP—ON THE RUSTED SEARCHLIGHT—NIGHT

A crude but **ICONIC BAT SYMBOL** BLAZES at its center—

> VOICE OVER
> We have a signal now... for
> when I'm needed...

REVEAL **A SILHOUETTED MAN** beside the light, waiting—

> VOICE OVER
> But when that light hits the sky,
> it's not just a call...

He's perched atop an **ABANDONED, HALF-BUILT SKYSCRAPER**—THE BRIGHT BEAM REACHES UPWARDS, sparkling in the rain—

> VOICE OVER
> It's a warning. To them...

OUTSIDE THE BODEGA

Sad Emoji BOLTS OUT toward a DARK ALLEY—when he spots TWO PEDESTRIANS GAPING UP AT THE SKY IN ALARM—he slows, peering up to SEE—**THE BAT-SIGNAL LOOMING**!

> VOICE OVER
> Fear is a tool...

Sad Emoji stops, <u>panic dawning</u> as he turns to the DARK ALLEY—he backs away, into the street—<u>a CAR SKIDS, HITTING HIM</u>! He DROPS—but fear lifts him, and <u>he just keeps running</u>—the sounds of a HELICOPTER grow as we—

EXT. COLOSSAL GOTHAM BANK—NIGHT

ON A VANDAL—hearing the copter, he peers up at—<u>A POLICE CHOPPER SOARING PAST **THE BAT-SIGNAL IN THE CLOUDS!**</u>

> VOICE OVER
> They think I'm hiding in the
> shadows...

He drops his spray can, startled as it CLATTERS! It rolls ominously under a DARK ARCHWAY—he stares, <u>chilled</u>—

> VOICE OVER
>
> But I <u>am</u> the shadows.

A SIREN APPROACHES—the VANDAL SPINS—joining
the others as THEY FLEE—we see the painted letters spell
"**BROKE!**" on the pillars; behind, A FIRE RAGES in the
building—FLAMES RISE as a MENACING LOW RUMBLE
BUILDS—and with a STARTLING BURST of METALLIC
SCREECHING, we—

EXT. ELEVATED TRAIN PLATFORM—POURING RAIN—NIGHT

The TRAIN SCREECHES TO A STOP—our Lone Passenger
emerges onto the deserted platform—when he hears
FOOTSTEPS and LAUGHTER behind—he TURNS, startled—

The <u>EIGHT SKULL FACED GANG MEMBERS are behind him.</u>
The Young Member stands coiled—a haunted look in his
eyes—the others watch with PHONES raised, filming—

> ONE OF THE MEMBERS
>
> <u>DO it, man</u>…!

He hesitates, losing nerve—and the Passenger BOLTS!

> THE LEADER
>
> <u>GET HIM!</u>

The GANG PLOWS FORWARD—KNOCKING the YOUNG
MEMBER DOWN as they RACE PAST—! THEY POUNCE ON
THE PASSENGER!

CLOSE ON THE YOUNG GANG MEMBER—the TRAIN
ROARING OFF beside him—WHEN HE SPOTS **THE BAT-
SIGNAL IN THE SKY!** His EYES DART around—AS
<u>SCREAMS APPROACH</u>; he turns—

The LEADER YANKS the YOUNG MEMBER to his feet—while the GROUP holds the PASSENGER—a DREADFUL SILENCE settling over the station as the train roar recedes...

THE LEADER
Now knock his ass out...

The Young Member stares, steeling himself—WHEN—

SLOW **BOOTSTEPS** ECHO from somewhere in the station—Everyone turns, looking anxiously around—THE YOUNG MAN'S EYES STARE into a DARK VOID beneath an overhang—THE OTHERS LOOK TOO—AS—CLICK... CLICK... CLICK...

A MASKED FIGURE SHROUDED IN BLACK APPEARS LIKE AN APPARITION FROM THE SHADOWS—STEPPING INTO THE RAIN—**IT'S THE BATMAN.**

Everyone stares, unnerved. The Leader smirks, sizing up what he assumes is just another Halloween costume—

THE LEADER
The hell are you supposed to be?

Batman stands there for a long, scary beat, eyes veiled:

THE BATMAN
I'm vengeance.

The unsettling effect of this response has barely an instant to register before BATMAN stalks for THE LEADER—

ONE OF THE GANG MEMBERS
Holy shit—it's him—!!!

THE LEADER raises his hands ready to fight—but totally unprepared for <u>this</u> fight—because—<u>BATMAN'S MOVEMENTS ARE INCONCEIVABLY BRUTAL AND FAST</u>—

The LEADER SWINGS—BATMAN SEIZES HIS ARM—a martial artist's savage grace—using his attacker's momentum to WRENCH HIM OFF BALANCE—SNAPPING HIS ARM SICKENINGLY—THE LEADER SCREAMS—as BATMAN SILENCES HIM AGAIN WITH A RAIN OF HEAD-SNAPPING JACKHAMMER PUNCHES IN THE FACE—<u>And like that, the Leader is down, bleeding, moaning</u>—

Batman looks up at the others, who gaze back, stunned— when a TRIO OF GANG MEMBERS RUSH HIM—CHAOS—as BATMAN DISPENSES WITH THEM <u>ALL AT ONCE</u> in a FLUID, BUT TOTALLY STREET-FIGHT REALISTIC ATTACK of KICKS and HARD FIST BLOWS—BATMAN TAKES HITS

TOO—but his TERRIFYING SKILL keeps impact from landing—HE'S LIKE A MACHINE—

Panic rips through the gang—the YOUNG MEMBER'S eyes widen as he SEES—SOMEONE **PULLING OUT A .38 SPECIAL**—

> YOUNG GANG MEMBER
> HEY MAN—NO—<u>NO</u>—!

BATMAN SPINS—SEEING THE GUN—<u>STARTS RIGHT FOR IT</u>—**THE GANG MEMBER OPENS FIRE**! BATMAN FLINCHES as the BULLETS DISAPPEAR into his suit's BALLISTIC FIBER—HE ADVANCES—GRABBING THE MEMBER'S STILL-FIRING GUN ARM IN ONE HAND—AND HIS THROAT IN THE OTHER—

AS THE GANG SCATTERS FROM THE BULLETS—A **BRIGHT BLUE TASER CURRENT ZAPS FROM BATMAN'S GLOVED FINGERS** INTO THE GANG MEMBERS NECK! The Gang Member <u>DROPS, CONVULSING!</u>

Batman slowly lifts his head, looking for more comers... The few remaining on their feet gape—<u>frozen</u>—Batman watches—as they BREAK INTO A RUN—all—EXCEPT—<u>the Youngest Gang Member</u>—who hesitates briefly under Batman's stone-faced gaze—<u>in awe</u>—then, races off...

Batman looks down to discover the Passenger, knocked to the ground in the chaos; he RAISES HIS HANDS, terrified—

> PASSENGER
> <u>...please don't hurt me...</u>

Batman just gazes strangely, cocking his head, taking a step slowly toward him—the Passenger BRACES HIMSELF—as

Batman PEERS DOWN at SOMETHING <u>BESIDE</u> THE PASSENGER'S HEAD—<u>a REFLECTION on the wet ground</u>—**THE BAT-SIGNAL!** Batman LOOKS UP—<u>wondering how long it's been there</u>—

INT. MAYOR'S TOWNHOUSE—MOVING DOWN THE HALL—NIGHT

FILLED WITH HUSHED COPS now; some turn as they NOTICE US, <u>STARING WITH HARSH EDGE</u>—**like what is <u>he</u> doing here?!**

REVEAL BATMAN, striding, unfazed, led by **<u>LIEUTENANT JAMES GORDON</u>**<u>, mid-40s</u>—<u>the Man we saw by the Bat-Signal</u>—

AT THE ENTRANCE TO THE STUDY

A UNIFORMED OFFICER steps into Batman's path—<u>ALARMED</u>—

> YOUNG OFFICER
> <u>Whoa-whoa-whoa</u>—police action—

Batman glares down at the Officer's hand on his chest—

> GORDON
> <u>He's with me, Officer</u>—

> YOUNG OFFICER
> Are ya—are ya <u>kiddin'</u> me, sir? You gonna let <u>him</u> in here...?

> GORDON
> Let him pass, Martinez.

The Officer turns in disbelief; steps aside—

> YOUNG OFFICER (MARTINEZ)
> ...goddamn freak...

THE STUDY

MITCHELL lies dead, HEAD MUMMIFIED IN DUCT TAPE—
over his mouth in red it says: "**NO MORE LIES**".
INVESTIGATORS TURN IN UTTER SHOCK at BATMAN
APPROACHING WITH GORDON—

> GORDON
> What do we know?

The LEAD is rattled as Batman stares at the body—

> GORDON
> Detective—

> LEAD DETECTIVE
> Sorry, Lieutenant... OK, yeah,
> we got... blunt-force trauma,
> lacerations on the head. He got
> hit alotta times, and hard.

> GORDON
> All this blood's from his head?

> LEAD DETECTIVE
> Most of it's from his hand—

CLOSE ON BATMAN staring, as the Detective LIFTS THE
HAND INTO FRAME, SOFT FOCUS FOREGROUND—showing
GORDON—

> LEAD DETECTIVE
> Thumb was severed. Killer may
> have taken it as a trophy—

> BATMAN
> <u>He was alive when it was cut off.</u>

Appalled, they turn to Batman, who stares at the hand—

> BATMAN
> Ecchymosis around the wound—

He rises to survey the area. Thrown by the interruption, the Detective watches him go—turns back to Gordon:

> DETECTIVE
> Security detail downstairs says
> the family was out trick-or-
> treating. Mayor was up here
> alone. Killer came through the
> skylight.

Batman sees a PHOTOGRAPHER flash a shot of BLOOD SPATTER on the FRAMED MARONI DRUG BUST HEADLINE on the wall—when Batman CLOCKS a <u>FRESH GASH IN THE WOOD FLOOR</u> (<u>the spot where the strange metal tool landed in our opening</u>).

He goes to examine it—the PHOTOGRAPHER suddenly noticing—it's a detail <u>he</u> obviously missed—as soon as Batman rises—he hustles over—SNAPS A SHOT—

> GORDON
> You said there was a <u>card</u>—

The Detective hands over AN ENVELOPE. Gordon pulls out a **HALLMARK-STYLE HALLOWEEN CARD**: a CREEPY SKELETON SMILES behind a WIDE-EYED OWL, tapping his shoulder—

> GORDON
> "From a secret friend... <u>Who</u>?"
>
> (opens card, reads)
> "Haven't a clue? Let's play a
> game, just me and you..."

Batman peers, as Gordon reads the KILLER'S SCRAWL—

> GORDON
> <u>"What does a liar do when he's</u>
> <u>dead?"</u>

WEIRD SYMBOLS ARE ETCHED at the bottom—Gordon pulls a PIECE OF PAPER from the envelope—**MORE WEIRD SYMBOLS**—

> GORDON
> There's a cipher too... Any of
> this... mean anything to you...?

Gordon pointedly shows Batman THE ENVELOPE—Batman <u>stares, struck</u>—but before he can speak—

> A QUIET, ALARMED VOICE (OS)
> <u>What's goin' on here?</u>

Everyone turns to see COMMISSIONER PETE SAVAGE, mid-50s—appalled at the sight of Batman—

> GORDON
> I asked him to come, Pete—

COMMISSIONER SAVAGE
This is a <u>crime scene</u>—it's
<u>Mitchell</u>, for Chrissakes—I got
<u>press</u> downstairs—!

(then, darker)
You know I cut you a <u>lotta</u> slack,
Jim, 'cuz we got history, but this
is <u>way</u> over the <u>line</u>...!

Gordon hands him the card; Savage reads in horror—when,
he sees THE ENVELOPE—<u>where he</u>—<u>and we</u>—<u>DISCOVER it's</u>
<u>addressed</u>: "**TO THE BATMAN**"—

COMMISSIONER SAVAGE
Wait—he's <u>involved</u> in this—?

GORDON
No, no—he's not involv—

COMMISSIONER SAVAGE
How do you <u>know</u>? He's a—he's a
goddamn <u>vigilante</u>—he could be

a <u>suspect</u>! Whattaya doing to
me—<u>we used to be partners</u>—

                    GORDON
Pete—I'm just looking for the
connection—

                    BATMAN (OS)
He lies still...

They turn—to see Batman, eyes fixed on the body—

                    COMMISSIONER SAVAGE
<u>Excuse me</u>—?

                    GORDON
                    (getting it, nodding)
The riddle. "What does a liar do
when he's dead"...? He lies still.

Unnerved by all this, Savage looks bitterly at Batman—

                    COMMISSIONER SAVAGE
Jesus... This must be your
favorite night of the year, huh
pal? Happy Fuckin' Halloween.

AN OFFICER appears in the doorway—

                    ANOTHER OFFICER
Excuse me, Commissioner—
they're ready for your
statement...

Savage sighs, nods—turns to Gordon, <u>deadly serious</u>—

COMMISSIONER SAVAGE
I want him outta here. Now.

And he leaves. As the POLICE ALL GLARE, Gordon starts to lead Batman out—but Batman stops, spotting something—a BLOODY FOOTPRINT, child sized—Gordon sees it, grim:

GORDON
Yeah, kid was the one found him.

Batman looks up at him disturbed: what kid...?

CUT TO:

THE LITTLE RED NINJA SITTING ON A BED IN A CHILD'S ROOM

Without his mask, we see now it's a TEN-YEAR-OLD BOY. We look through the doorway at him as he stares down, lost, surrounded by COPS. Finally, he LOOKS UP at us—

REVEAL BATMAN gazing back through the doorway. As MORE COPS BEGIN TO NOTICE HIM—Gordon, beside him, WHISPERS:

GORDON
We... really gotta go, man...

Batman nods, but stays a moment longer—the aching, opening chords of **NIRVANA'S "SOMETHING IN THE WAY"** BEGIN; HOLD as Batman stares from somewhere under that mask... an unspoken connection to this newly fatherless boy...

COMMISSIONER SAVAGE
(PRELAP)
Tonight, a son lost a father...

EXT. MAYOR'S MANSION—FRONT STEPS—PRE-DAWN

A press conference; MITCHELL'S WIFE cries behind Savage—

>   COMMISSIONER SAVAGE
>   ...a wife lost a husband. And I
>   lost a friend. Mayor Mitchell was
>   a fighter for our city and I won't
>   rest until this killer is found...

As NIRVANA CONTINUES—

DISTANT PERSPECTIVE ON THE PRESS CONFERENCE—SAME MOMENT

An ENGINE PURRS; PULL BACK TO REVEAL we're LOOKING PAST A FIGURE—**THE DRIFTER**. He watches from the shadows across the street on an old, unpainted CAFE RACER MOTORCYCLE; he pulls on a HELMET... CLOSE ON the dark, full face visor—

>   VOICE OVER
>   I wish I could say I'm making a
>   difference... but I don't know...

EXT. GOTHAM—MOVING THROUGH THE STREETS—PRE-DAWN

NIRVANA SWELLS as we CHASE the BIKE through LOWER GOTHAM; the PRESS CONFERENCE BLAZES on DECAYING JUMBOTRONS—

>   VOICE OVER
>   Murder, robberies, assault—two
>   years later, they're all up... And
>   now this...

—PASSING TENT CITIES, HALTED CONSTRUCTION SITES
UNDER SIGNS: "**A GOTHAM RENEWAL PROJECT**"—
PLASTERED OVER SOME ARE BELLA REÁL CAMPAIGN
BILLS: "**TIME FOR A REAL CHANGE**"—

> VOICE OVER
> The city's eating itself... Maybe
> it's beyond saving...

—ALONG ONE OF THE BRIDGES SPANNING THE ISLANDS
OF GOTHAM—SKYLINE BEHIND—A MASSIVE **SEA WALL**
BELOW—

> VOICE OVER
> But I have to try. <u>Push myself</u>...

—UNTIL WE SOAR OVER THE BIKE AS IT TEARS THROUGH
A ROLLING CITY PARK—DOWN A NARROW ROAD—

DISAPPEARING INTO A TUNNEL UNDER A BEAUTIFUL, ARCHING BRIDGE—WE TIP UP TOWARD THE DISTANCE, TO SEE IT'S HEADING TOWARD—A GOTHIC 1920s BUILDING BELOW THE PARK: **WAYNE TOWER**—

INT. NARROW, OLD TUNNEL—PRE-DAWN

The bike rips down a secret passage from a bygone era—

INTO THE UNDERGROUND FOUNDATION OF WAYNE TOWER

The Drifter SKIDS to a stop, HUNDREDS OF CREATURES all along the rock ceiling STIR ANXIOUSLY TO LIFE—**BATS**...

> VOICE OVER
> These nights all roll together, in
> a rush... behind the mask...

...as he removes his helmet—and we finally SEE **BRUCE WAYNE**—handsome, 30, black camo still around his eyes.

CUT TO:

SUPER-TIGHT—FINGERS REMOVING CONTACT LENSES— ON THE CURVED SURFACE OF THE LENSES ARE TINY SENSOR BANDS—

> VOICE OVER
> Sometimes, in the morning, I
> have to force myself to
> remember...

CLOSE ON GRAINY VIDEO FOOTAGE—the gang member from last night LOOKS AT US as he gets tased in the neck—

> VOICE OVER
> ...everything that happened.

CLOSE ON A HANDWRITTEN JOURNAL—PHRASES: **"THURSDAY, OCT. 31"**—**"NOCTURNAL ANIMAL"**—**"PUSH MYSELF"**—a PEN FINISHES the entry—as the journal shuts, we see THE COVER: **"NOTES & OBSERVATIONS (GOTHAM PROJECT) YR. 2"**

REVEAL BRUCE—HIGH ANGLE OVER **"THE CAVE"**—EARLY MORNING

NIRVANA ECHOES as Bruce REVIEWS FOOTAGE at a work bench in a giant boiler room turned survivalist chop shop—PROJECTS IN VARIOUS STATES, including **A HALF-BUILT, BLACK MUSCLE CAR**, both retro and like nothing we've ever seen. A TV plays GC1; the headline, **"MAYOR MITCHELL MURDERED"**—below it: "ACTING MAYOR TOMLIN TO RUN IN HIS PLACE"

> **GC1 NEWSCASTER**
> ...this certainly isn't the first time Gotham has been rocked by the murder of a political figure. In fact, in an eerie coincidence it was twenty years ago this month that celebrated billionaire philanthropist, Dr. Thomas Wayne, and his wife Martha were slain during Wayne's own mayoral campaign in a shocking crime that remains unsolved to this day—

Bruce's eyes go to the TV; when from the FREIGHT ELEVATOR steps ALFRED, 50s, muscular, waistcoat and shirtsleeves—he walks on an elegant CANE, SCAR on his face, eyes on the

TV—seeing him, Bruce resumes work—Alfred turns to Bruce—an unspoken tension; Bruce avoids his gaze—

                    ALFRED
          I assume you heard about this...?

                    BRUCE
     Yeah.

Alfred suddenly notices the CONTACTS LENS MURDER SCENE FOOTAGE Bruce is hi-speeding through—moves closer—

                    ALFRED
     <u>Oh</u>. I see...

               (off Mitchell's body)
          ...dear God...

As the CIPHER fills the screen, Bruce FREEZES the image, PRINTING it—Alfred looks chilled—as Bruce works—

                    ALFRED
          The killer left this <u>for Batman</u>?

                    BRUCE
     Apparently.

                    ALFRED
          You're becoming quite a
          celebrity.

          ...why is he writing to <u>you</u>?

                    BRUCE
     I don't know yet.

ALFRED

Have a shower. The accounting
boys from Wayne Enterprises
are coming for breakfast.

BRUCE

Here—why—?

ALFRED

Because I couldn't get you to go
there—

BRUCE

I don't have time for this.

ALFRED
(a tense beat)
It's getting serious, Bruce. If this
continues, it won't be long
before you've nothing left—

BRUCE

I don't care about that. Any of
that.

ALFRED

...you don't care about your
family's legacy?

BRUCE

What I'm doing is my family's
legacy—and if I can't change
things here, if I can't have an
effect, then I don't care what
happens to me—

ALFRED

That's what I'm afraid of—

BRUCE

Stop. You're not my father,
Alfred.

ALFRED
(a thin smile)
I'm... well aware.

Bruce rises—Alfred watches him go, pained. Then turns to
the computer, seeing THUMBNAILS from the lens footage;
one is THE BOY IN NINJA COSTUME. He clicks it; the boy
looks up, sad. Alfred stares, deeply affected.

Alfred's eyes drift to the PRINTED CIPHER. His gaze fixes on
words Bruce has written above the eerie symbols in the
Halloween card: "**HE LIES STILL**"...

INT. WAYNE TOWER—GRAND FOYER—MOVING—MORNING

Atop the staircase, we start on a SET OF DOUBLE DOORS—
a THICK CHAIN coiled crudely through the handles, a
PADLOCK sealing us off from whatever is beyond—Bruce
moves past, down stairs, wet hair, pulling on a t-shirt—
muscular but underweight like a rock star—a street fighter's
scars and bruises—MOVE with him, through the apartment's
hotel-like scale—and neglect that has left dirt and disrepair
over former grandeur—he ENTERS—

THE DINING ROOM

—to find Alfred at the table, immersed in what looks like a
crossword—without looking up, Alfred points—

ALFRED

Some fresh berries there...

Bruce squints, unaccustomed to morning; grabbing berries, he pulls out sunglasses—when he sees Alfred's working on the CIPHER; Alfred's interest breaks the ice—

BRUCE

...what're you doing?

ALFRED

Just reminiscing about my days in the Circus. This is actually quite... elusive.

BRUCE

Where'd you get the O's?

ALFRED

"He lies still" is only a partial key. It only gives us H, E, L, I, and S—so I'm looking for any double symbols to start, trying letters, see where it leads...

BRUCE

Interesting.

An ELDERLY MAID appears in the doorway—

ELDERLY MAID

The gentlemen are here.

Alfred discreetly closes his newspaper over the cipher—

ALFRED

See them in please, Dory...

THE DINING ROOM—MOMENTS LATER

TWO YOUNG EXECUTIVES STARE RIGHT AT US—

> ONE OF THE EXECUTIVES
> I'm afraid we're at a critical
> point here—

REVEAL BRUCE—in SUNGLASSES, stone-faced—his gaze
shifts distractedly to Alfred's newspaper on the table—

> ONE OF THE EXECUTIVES
> At the very least, we'll need your
> signature to cover these losses...

Bruce reaches for the newspaper, opens it—the execs glance
at each other, thrown; Alfred smiles, apologetic—Bruce
stares at the SEA OF LETTERS, wheels turning—

> ONE OF THE EXECUTIVES (OS)
> Mr. Wayne...?

> BRUCE
> (glances blankly up)
> ...what?

> YOUNG EXECUTIVE
> I... I need your signature, sir...

And as Bruce signs—we PRELAP:

> BRUCE (VO)
> What if it isn't a partial key...?

BACK IN "THE CAVE"—MINUTES LATER

Bruce and Alfred work on the cipher on Bruce's computer—

ALFRED

What do you mean?

BRUCE

What if it's the <u>whole</u> key?
<u>Ignore</u> the symbols we don't
have letters for, use only the
letters from "he lies still", and
leave the rest—

ALFRED

—blank, yes—I understand—

(deleting letters)
—but that will leave <u>most</u> of the
cipher unsolved... I don't see
how that—<u>oh</u>...

(suddenly impressed)
Well.

They gaze at THE LAPTOP: most of the cipher is now blank,
<u>but the remaining letters line up like connect-the-dots to</u>
<u>form A SINGLE HUGE WORD across the page:</u> "**D R I V E**"

**INT. GOTHAM CITY POLICE DEPARTMENT—COMMAND
CENTER—DAY**

The room bustles with POLICE and FBI CODEBREAKERS, all
fixated on the CIPHER, projected huge on the wall. One of the
G.C.P.D. DETECTIVES quietly briefs Gordon—

DETECTIVE

Feds say code could take
weeks—if they can crack it
<u>at all</u>—

Gordon's cell rings; he looks: "<u>NO CALLER ID</u>"; answers—

BRUCE (VO)
<u>Did Mitchell have a car</u>—?

GORDON
I'm sorry, can you hold on,
honey?

(to Detective)
My daughter, Barbara—

The Detective nods as Gordon takes a few steps away—

GORDON
(into phone, low)
A car? Yeah, I'm sure—why...?

INT. MAYOR'S MANSION—FREIGHT ELEVATOR—NIGHT

Batman and Gordon descend in DARKNESS—after a beat,
Gordon steals a look, studying the visible part of Batman's
face—Batman feels it, turns—Gordon looks away—they stare
forward again as the DOORS OPEN to—

**A SUBTERRANEAN GARAGE FILLED WITH PRICELESS EXOTIC
CARS—**

They walk out, scanning the maze of stunning vehicles...

GORDON
<u>Damn</u>. Where do we even
<u>start</u>...?

(eyeing the cars)
You sure this isn't a leap?

"Drive" could mean anything...

> BATMAN
> You don't trust me?

> GORDON
> Trust you? You mean like you trust <u>me</u>? It's been two years, I still don't even know who you are, man—

> BATMAN
> <u>There...</u>

Gordon looks at an ASTON DB11: <u>one of the tires is flat</u>. They approach. Batman kneels, pulling a PAIR OF POULTRY SHEARS out of the tire—<u>they're COVERED IN DRIED BLOOD</u>.

INSIDE THE DB11

Batman turns on a UV LIGHT BAR—searching the console—

> GORDON
> What're we looking for—?

> BATMAN
> ...USB port—

> GORDON
> —<u>USB</u>—?

Batman stops, struck. Looks at Gordon, who can't see inside the console—then looks back—

> GORDON
> <u>What</u>...?

Batman pulls out a **KEY RING USB DRIVE**—attached to it, in a little clear plastic bag, is a **SEVERED THUMB**...

                    BATMAN
          Thumb. Drive.

                    GORDON
     Jesus.

OUTSIDE THE ASTON DB11—SECONDS LATER

They stare at Gordon's field laptop—as it BEEPS—

                    GORDON
          It's encrypted.

                    BATMAN (OS)
        Try this...

Gordon turns... Batman holds up THE BAG WITH THE SEVERED THUMB. Gordon sighs, taking it—shakes his head, presses the thumb to the drive—it OPENS—

                    GORDON
          Boy, this guy's hilarious.

SURVEILLANCE PHOTOS pop up: Mayor Mitchell exiting a seedy nightclub with a TWENTY-TWO YEAR OLD IN CLUBWEAR, headed for his Aston DB11, a black eye visible under the Woman's sunglasses; behind them follow UNSAVORY TYPES, a gangster vibe—one wears a STREET-STYLED, STRIPED TUX—

                    GORDON
          ...so much for family values.

                    BATMAN
          ...who is she?

                    GORDON
          No idea... But that's The
          Penguin—Carmine Falcone's
          right hand—

                    BATMAN
          —I know who he is.

When—a WHOOSH! sound suddenly emits from the laptop!

                    GORDON
          —what was that—?

                    GORDON
               (clicking windows)
          Shit-shit-shit—

                    BATMAN
          What—?

                    GORDON
          The mail app—it just—it, it sent
          out the photos! Goddammit!

          Gotham Post, Gazette, GC1!
          Jesus—I'm gonna have to go deal
          with this, Pete's gonna hit the
          roof.

                    BATMAN
               (looks at photos)
          "He lies still"... About her?

> GORDON

>Maybe... That's the Iceberg
>Lounge—it's under the
>Shoreline Lofts where Falcone's
>holed up. We'll never get in
>without a warrant.

> BATMAN

> (won't stop him)
>...yeah...

EXT. ICEBERG LOUNGE NIGHTCLUB—MOVING SHOT—NIGHT

PUSHING toward a deserted warehouse—a nondescript door
in the facade; a LONE SODIUM STREETLAMP FLICKERS,
illuminating an old sign: ICEBERG FISH CO—as BAT-BOOTS
CLICK purposefully into frame—

BLACKNESS

SWINGS OPEN to reveal Batman in shadow; CLUB MUSIC
booms:

> BATMAN

>Know who I am?

A HUGE BOUNCER'S eyes give the Bat-suit the once over—

> BOUNCER

>Yeah, I got an idea.

> BATMAN

>I wanna see The Penguin.

> BOUNCER

>Penguin? I don't know what
>you're talking about, pal.

Batman just stares. The Bouncer shuts the door. A beat, then it opens again. Now there are two of them—<u>TWINS</u>.

> IDENTICAL TWIN BOUNCER
> What's the problem?

> BOUNCER
> Says he wants to see The Penguin.

> IDENTICAL TWIN BOUNCER
> <u>Penguin</u>? Ain't no Penguin here—

> BOUNCER
> That's what I tried to <u>tell</u> him—

> IDENTICAL TWIN BOUNCER
> Get <u>outta</u> here, freak. Ya <u>hear</u> me? Or that little suit's gonna get all full of blood.

Batman remains eerily still.

> BATMAN
> Mine? Or yours?

The Twin LUNGES—blind-sided by Batman's VICIOUS ELBOW STRIKE—the other Twin CHARGES—his throat meets the HEEL OF BATMAN'S PALM—and just like that, WE'RE—

FOLLOWING BATMAN INSIDE (IN A CONTINUOUS HANDHELD SHOT)

MUSIC THROBS as we plunge down A CORRIDOR—CIRCLING BATMAN—BEHIND HIM we see THE TWINS staggering

back in—SCREAMING to alert MORE BOUNCERS—<u>who
SCRAMBLE as</u>—Batman emerges onto the landing above the
club—strobe lights reveal glimpses of SHOWGIRLS ABOVE A
DANCE FLOOR—

Batman starts downstairs—when the BOUNCERS
POUNCE—A MARTIAL ARTS BRAWL ERUPTING as they
descend—Batman taking on TWO AT A TIME—CRACKING
HEADS ON RAILINGS—until he LEAPS OVER ONE—
dropping a full story!

—Batman spots <u>ANOTHER BOUNCER with an ALUMINUM
BAT</u>—who SWINGS—Batman STEPS IN FAST—THROWING
AN ELBOW—TWISTING THE BAT FREE—DROPPING THE
BOUNCER HARD—

<u>A MUSTACHED BOUNCER PULLS A **GUN**—**BATMAN
TWIRLS THE BAT**</u> under STROBE LIGHTS—MUSTACHE

FIRES—BULLETS PING OFF THE BAT—BATMAN LETS IT FLY—<u>KNOCKING MUSTACHE OUT!</u>

BATMAN SEES **THE TWINS**—BACK AGAIN—ONE HAS A SHOTGUN—<u>CLUBBERS SHRIEK—AS BATMAN TRIGGERS</u> **A QUICK-DRAW SLIDER ON HIS ARM**—WHIPPING **A HARPOON GUN** TO HIS FIST—<u>FIRING THROUGH THE GUNMAN'S LEGS INTO HIS BROTHER'S FOOT BEHIND HIM—THE LINE RETRACTS—YANKING HIM FORWARD—UPENDING THEM BOTH—the GUN FIRES into the ceiling!</u>

The club in TOTAL CHAOS now—<u>when **SOMEONE** comes up behind</u>—BATMAN SPINS, ready for more—**TO SEE A MAN WITH A MISSHAPED NOSE IN A STRIPED TUX AND LAVENDER BOW TIE**—he puts his hands up—grinning—in awe—

> THE PENGUIN
> Whoa-whoa-whoa—take it easy,
> sweetheart! You lookin' for <u>me</u>?
> See you met the twins. Boy,
> you're everything they say,
> aren't you?
>
> (smiles big, flashing a shiny gold tooth)
> Guess we both are. Howya doin'?
> I'm Oz.

He hobbles closer on a CLUBBED FOOT—sticks out a hand to shake—Batman doesn't return the gesture—

INT. DIM CLUB DRESSING ROOM/BACKROOM OFFICE AREA— NIGHT

At a desk enclosed by racks of showgirl costumes, Penguin looks at THE PHOTO OF THE TWENTY-TWO YEAR OLD AND MAYOR—

> BATMAN
> Who is she?

> THE PENGUIN
> I really don't know, chief—I mighta been comin' out same time but I wasn't rollin' with them—

FOOTSTEPS interrupt—through a gap in costumes, Batman spies **A FIGURE IN A HIGH-SLIT EVENING GOWN**—a STUNNING WOMAN appears—streetwise vibe. She stops, uneasy—

> THE PENGUIN
> No, no—it's OK, baby—Mr. Vengeance here don't bite...

She hesitates, eyes on Batman; then saunters to Penguin, sets down a drink tray; as Penguin touches her thigh, she slyly brushes his hand away with a smile—says low—

> WOMAN IN THE EVENING GOWN
> Touch me again, Oz, I'll break those stubby little fingers, OK?

> THE PENGUIN
> What? The dress, I was just feelin' the material—sorry...!

He lifts AN ENVELOPE OF CASH off the tray—Batman watches him hand the Woman A RUBBER-BANDED CLUSTER OF VIALS WITH EYE-DROPPERS—a.k.a. "**DROPS**"—the Woman turns to go, but stops, struck, as she sees THE PHOTO—her eyes briefly meet Batman's—then she heads out—

> BATMAN
> (points to photo)
> I wanna know who she is, and what she has to do with his murder?

> THE PENGUIN
> Whose murder—?

> BATMAN
> The mayor—

> THE PENGUIN
> —is that the mayor? Oh shit, it is, lookit that—!

Batman YANKS HIM from his seat, SLAMS HIM INTO A MIRROR!

> BATMAN
> Don't make me hurt you.

> THE PENGUIN
> You better watch it... You know my reputation?

> BATMAN
> Yeah, I do. Do you?

Anger flares suddenly in Penguin's eyes—a nerve struck. Finally, he pushes it down, smiling, evasive.

THE PENGUIN

Look, I'm just a proprietor, OK?
What people do here ain't got
nothin' to do with me.

Batman senses something in the mirror—he turns—<u>to see the
Woman in the Evening Gown still watching through the
doorway in the distance</u>—she disappears again—

THE PENGUIN

I'll tell ya one thing...

Batman turns back—Penguin hands him the photo—

THE PENGUIN

Whoever she is, she's one hot
chick.

(smiles cruelly)
Why don't you ask Mitchell's
<u>wife</u>? Maybe <u>she</u> knows.

(off Batman's look)
What? Too soon?

Batman looks at the photo again—<u>spots an Evening Gown in
the b.g.</u>—<u>face in shadow, but there's no mistaking that dress</u>—
as Batman moves for the empty doorway—

THE PENGUIN (OS)

You let me know there's
anything else I can do! OK,
sunshine?!

OUTSIDE THE OFFICE

Batman stops, looking around—<u>the Woman is gone</u>.

EXT. ICEBERG LOUNGE NIGHTCLUB—POURING RAIN NOW— LATER

The Woman emerges in a coat, looking anxiously for a cab under the FLICKERING STREET LAMP, flags down a NAVY GYPSY CAB—hand-painted on the door: "We're Not Yellow—We Go Anywhere". She gets in. PAN with the cab as it speeds off... right by a HELMETED MOTORCYCLIST— **THE DRIFTER**.

INT. NAVY BLUE GYPSY CAB—BACKSEAT—LATE NIGHT

The Woman on her cell—speaks low as someone picks up:

> WOMAN IN THE EVENING GOWN
> Hey, it's me. Whatsa matter,
> baby?—slow down, I can't... On
> the news? No, wait for me, I'm
> on my way home! We're gonna
> get the hell outta here, I promise,
> if we have to go sooner, we'll
> go tonight!

HOLD on her worried face as FOCUS DRIFTS through the rear window to REVEAL THE HELMETED **DRIFTER,** FOLLOWING HER...

EXT. RUN-DOWN, EAST END APARTMENT—BINOCULAR POV— NIGHT

QUIET BREATHING as BINOCULARS SEARCH THE FACADE—LIGHTS COME ON IN THE SECOND STORY—THE WOMAN, entering HER APARTMENT—CATS SWARM HER as she rushes to THE KITCHEN—finding a YOUNG WOMAN WITH A BRUISED FACE, eyes on the TV—who grows hysterical, gesturing to the **PHOTOS OF THE MAYOR AND THE TWENTY-TWO YEAR OLD** playing on GC1—and as the Woman in the Gown tries to calm her, we see: **THE BRUISED YOUNG WOMAN IS THE TWENTY-TWO YEAR OLD**—

REVEAL **THE DRIFTER** (BRUCE HIDDEN IN CAP AND ARMY JACKET)

—watching through binoculars FROM A NEARBY ROOFTOP—

THE BINOCULAR POV

FOLLOWS the Woman in Evening Gown to a BATHROOM; she opens a cabinet, getting PILLS—then rushes back to THE KITCHEN—distraught, the Bruised Woman takes them—the Woman in Gown caresses her head—the Bruised Woman pushes her away, inconsolable. The Woman in Gown stands, at a loss. Then, resolve building, marches off—BINOCULARS FOLLOWING as she—and all her cats—head into a BEDROOM—where she stealthily shuts the door—we watch IN SILHOUETTE as she slips out of her dress... and begins sliding into **A SKIN-TIGHT, BLACK LEATHER BODYSUIT**... as her cats nuzzle against her legs...

THE DRIFTER GAZES, STRUCK BY THE SIGHT OF THE WOMAN, AS—

THE "CATWOMAN"

climbs nimbly out to the fire escape—swinging like an acrobat to the ground below; she ducks into the garage—

THE DRIFTER LOWERS THE GLASSES, ALARMED HE'LL LOSE HER—

EXT. EAST END APARTMENT—GARAGE FRONT—MOMENTS LATER

A BLACK SPORT BIKE appears—<u>THE HELMETED CATWOMAN ROARS onto the street</u>—PAST **THE DRIFTER** getting on <u>his</u> bike—

EXT. GOTHAM STREETS—MOVING SUPER FAST—NIGHT

<u>THROTTLING HARD through traffic to keep CATWOMAN in sight</u>—as she WEAVES in and out of view a hundred feet ahead—<u>SLALOMING CARS—THE DRIFTER RACES JUST TO KEEP PACE!</u>

INT. MAYOR'S MANSION—LOOKING UP AT SKYLIGHT—NIGHT

A FIGURE LOWERS GRACEFULLY on a rope—<u>THE CATWOMAN</u>—

INT. MAYOR'S MANSION—STUDY—THE CRIME SCENE— NIGHT

She prowls, a BLACK MOTORCYCLE WIND MASK over her face—finds <u>A WALL SAFE</u>—working tumblers till... it's open—

> A VOICE (OS)
> You're pretty good at that...

<u>She turns to see</u> **BATMAN IN SHADOW**—she GRABS SOMETHING FROM THE SAFE—BREAKS for the door—he STALKS AFTER, GRABS her—she SPINS, SWINGING A VICIOUS ROUNDHOUSE—surprised, he RECOILS, blocking **BLINDING KICK AFTER KICK** with raised arms—<u>SHE'S REALLY GODDAMN GOOD!</u>

Her BRUTAL ASSAULT drives him back—when suddenly— he TWISTS, GRABBING HER LEG—they CRASH over the

desk—and suddenly she's on her back—he reaches down—SNATCHING whatever she stole—an **ESTONIAN PASSPORT**—

> CATWOMAN
> Hey—!

Batman opens it: it belongs to **THE TWENTY-TWO YEAR OLD**—

> BATMAN
> Kosolov, Annika—

> CATWOMAN
> Gimme that—

                    BATMAN
          He hurt her? That why you
          killed him?

                    CATWOMAN
          What?! Oh, please—just gimme
          the goddamn—!

She LUNGES for the passport—as Batman WRAPS AROUND
HER—pulling her down BEHIND THE DESK—she's
bewildered—when she sees **A FLASHLIGHT** spilling through
the doorway—it's **A SECURITY COP** arriving to investigate
the noise... he scans the scene—as they wait, bodies pressed
close—her eyes swim as Batman holds her... Satisfied, the Cop
leaves—Catwoman shrugs Batman off, hard—standing—

                    CATWOMAN
          Listen, honey—you got the
          wrong idea, OK? I didn't kill
          anybody—I'm here for my
          friend. She's tryin'a get the hell
          outta here—this sonuvabitch
          had her passport.

                    BATMAN
          What does she know?

                    CATWOMAN
          Whatever it is, it's got her so
          scared she won't even tell me.

                    BATMAN
                    (wry)
          She did seem upset...

She looks at him, confused. He stares back, provocative:

> BATMAN
> Back at your place.

She can't believe it: He was there...?

> BATMAN
> Let's go talk to her.

Finally, he offers the passport... She glares at it...

EXT. WET GOTHAM STEETS—NIGHT

Batman and Catwoman jockey for the lead on their bikes—THEY ROCKET PAST at over 100 mph—**A FLEETING BLUR**—we LAND ON TWO STUNNED PEDESTRIANS, craning their heads—

INT. SELINA'S APARTMENT—NIGHT

THE PLACE HAS BEEN RANSACKED—Batman and Catwoman enter—distraught, she rushes deeper into the apartment—

> CATWOMAN (OS)
> Anni! Baby...?!

Batman examines the scene—hears the TV—moves to—

THE DIM KITCHEN

—sees UNPAID BILLS on the counter—picks one up, sees the name: SELINA KYLE—when the TV steals his attention—THE GC1 HEADLINE: "**SERIAL KILLER CLAIMS CREDIT**

FOR SECOND VICTIM IN TWO DAYS—GCPD COMMISSIONER MURDERED"

Catwoman comes in, now deeply rattled—guilty—

>   CATWOMAN
> Jesus, what are they going to do
> to her? She's just a kid. And now
> they know who I am too, they
> took my phone, everything—

—she notices Batman grimly staring, turns to THE TV—

>   NEWSCASTER (ON TV)
> ...the killer posted the following
> message on social media. We
> should warn you, the video is
> disturbing.

A HANDHELD VIDEO begins—a SELFIE of THE OLIVE GREEN HOODED KILLER we saw in the opening—a new SYMBOL on his chest: a **SCRAWLED QUESTION MARK WITHIN CROSSHAIRS**—

>   MASKED MAN
>   (eerie VOICE CHANGER)
> Hello, people of Gotham... This...
> is the The Riddler speaking. On
> Halloween night, I killed your
> mayor, because he was not who
> he pretended to be. But I am not
> done. Here... is another...

He swings the camera to A BOUND, NAKED MAN WITH **A CAGE-LIKE BOX OVER HIS HEAD**—the camera presses in to see COMMISSIONER SAVAGE INSIDE, mouth covered in duct tape and words: "NO MORE LIES" —**FERAL RATS** circle his face—

> MASKED MAN/THE RIDDLER (OS)
> ...who will soon... be losing <u>face</u>...
> I will kill again and again, until
> our Day of Judgement... when
> the Truth about our city will
> finally be Unmasked.

> (leans into view)
> GOOD Byeee...

And as we hear MUFFLED SHRIEKS—the video abruptly ENDS—a smiling press photo of Commissioner Savage appears—

> CATWOMAN
> Holy shit... I seen that guy too.
> At the club.

> BATMAN
> The Iceberg Lounge?

> CATWOMAN
> The 44 Below.

> (off his look)
> The club within the club—the <u>real</u> club. It's a mob hangout.

> BATMAN
> That where you work? Selina?

> CATWOMAN
> (turns, struck; then)
> I work at the bar, upstairs. <u>But I
> see them come in.</u>

                    BATMAN
        Who?

                    CATWOMAN
        Everybody. Lotta guys who
        shouldn't be there, I can tell you
        that. Your basic upstanding
        citizen types.

                    BATMAN
        You're gonna help me on this.
        For your friend.

She warily studies his eyes, when Batman feels something at
his feet—a swarm of cats—he looks at her—

                    BATMAN
        You got a lotta cats.

                    CATWOMAN
        I have a thing about strays.

                    BATMAN
            (starts to go)
        You're not safe here.

                    CATWOMAN
        I can take care of myself...

But he just keeps going. She turns grimly to the TV—

                NEWSCASTER (ON TV)
        ...with two public figures now
        dead in just the last two nights,
        and only days before the
        election, police and city officials

are left searching for a killer,
and hoping to find him <u>before he
kills again</u>.

BLACKNESS

SLIDES OPEN—SCREECHING INTO LIGHT—we LOOK UP at
FLARING FLUORESCENTS as BATMAN AND GORDON PEER
DOWN AT US. Gordon has to look away—Batman coldly
assesses—

> **GORDON**
> He waited for him. At the gym.
> Pete liked to work out late at
> night when nobody was around.

> **BATMAN**
> <u>Needle mark on his neck</u>...

> GORDON
> Sonuvabitch injected him with
> arsenic.

> BATMAN
> Rat poison.

> GORDON
> That seems to be his theme here.

As Gordon steps angrily away—we finally REVEAL—

THE MEDICAL EXAMINER'S ROOM

SAVAGE'S BODY on a MORGUE DRAWER—Batman follows
Gordon to an EVIDENCE TABLE... sees the **CREEPY, HINGED,
CAGE-LIKE HEAD BOX**—inside is an elaborate network of
channels—

> BATMAN
> ...it's a maze.

> GORDON
> Kinda sicko does this to a
> person?

Gordon gazes inside the bloody MAZE, where a crudely
PAINTED CIPHER ends on a QUESTION MARK IN
CROSSHAIRS—as Batman finds a stack of SURVEILLANCE
PHOTOS—

> GORDON
> He blasted those out after his
> message went viral. This guy
> murders you and your
> reputation.

In one of the photos: the COMMISSIONER emerges from the Iceberg Lounge, SHAKES HANDS with a SHADY GUY—

> BATMAN
> Guy pushes drops. On the East
> End.

Gordon looks on, pained, as Batman stares at another photo: SAVAGE PEEKING INTO A CASH-STUFFED ENVELOPE—

> GORDON
> I don't get it. Why would Pete
> get involved in this?

> BATMAN
> Looks like he got greedy.

> GORDON
> Are you kidding? After
> everything we did to bust up the
> Maronis? We shut down their
> whole operation—now he's
> caving to some dealer?

> BATMAN
> Maybe he's not who you
> thought—

> GORDON
> You make it sound like he had it
> coming—

> BATMAN
> He was a cop. He crossed the
> line.

Gordon sighs—when Batman NOTICES SOMETHING TAPED TO THE BACK OF THE HEAD BOX—AN ENVELOPE: **"TO THE BATMAN"**

Gordon watches Batman open it: ANOTHER GREETING CARD. A CARTOON SCIENTIST mixes beakers: **"I'm MAD About You! Want to Know My Name? Just Look Inside and See…"** Inside is A CARTOON EXPLOSION; over it: **"But, Wait, I Cannot Tell You—It Might Spoil the Chemistry!"** He reads the SCRIBBLE:

> BATMAN
> "Follow the maze till you find
> the rat—bring him into the light,
> and you'll find where I'm at."

> GORDON
> The hell's all that—Bring him
> into the light? Find the rat?

Unnerved, Batman stares at HIS NAME on the envelope—

> BATMAN
> …I don't know…

INT. VISITING CELL—ARKHAM PRISON FOR THE INSANE—NIGHT

A ROLL-UP DOOR rises behind GLASS as Batman waits; we glimpse THE PRISONER'S PALE HANDS and JUMPSUIT, **BUT HIS FACE REMAINS HIDDEN THROUGH THE SCENE**. BATMAN glares; he puts A FILE in the partition drawer, pushes it through…

> UNSEEN PRISONER'S VOICE
> (smile in his voice)
> A present. Almost our
> anniversary, isn't it?

                    BATMAN
        There's a serial killer. I want
        your perspective.

The PRISONER'S FINGERS stroke the cover as he considers.

              UNSEEN PRISONER'S VOICE
        First anniversary _is_ paper.

                    (then)
        What makes you think I come so
        cheap?

                    BATMAN
        I thought you'd be curious.

              UNSEEN PRISONER'S VOICE
        Oh, a little lurid reading. You
        think I get off on this stuff.

                    BATMAN
        Don't you?

              UNSEEN PRISONER'S VOICE
        ...you have _pictures_?

Batman just stares; the Prisoner looks at the file...

              UNSEEN PRISONER'S VOICE
        Oh, his violence is so... _baroque_.
        He likes little _puzzles_, doesn't
        he? So meticulous. It's like he's
        been planning this _his whole_
        life.

                    (then, a quiet taunt)
        I know who he is.

                         BATMAN
          Who?

The PRISONER'S BLURRED FACE just stares back,
hauntingly.

                         BATMAN
          Who is he?

              UNSEEN PRISONER'S VOICE
          He's a nobody. Who wants to be
          somebody. The mayor. The
          commissioner. He's got
          ambition.

                         BATMAN
          You think his motive's political?

              UNSEEN PRISONER'S VOICE
          No. This is... very personal. He
          feels these people have all
          wronged him. Probably goes
          way back... Unhealed wounds,
          stolen lunch money...

                         BATMAN
          Why's he writing to me?

              UNSEEN PRISONER'S VOICE
          Maybe he's a fan. Or maybe he's
          got a grudge against you too.
          Maybe you're the main course.
          Any theories? I'm sure you have
          your own hypothesis.

                    BATMAN
Not yet.

                    UNSEEN PRISONER'S VOICE
<u>Really</u>? You're normally so
ahead of the curve. But
something's different this time.
This is... very <u>upsetting</u> to you—

                    BATMAN
Let's get back to him—

                    UNSEEN PRISONER'S VOICE
Why? You're so much more
<u>fun</u>—

                    BATMAN
<u>I'm not here to talk about me</u>—

                    UNSEEN PRISONER'S VOICE
What <u>are</u> you here to talk about?

                    BATMAN
<u>I wanna know how he thinks</u>—

                    UNSEEN PRISONER'S VOICE
Oh, come on—<u>you</u> know
<u>exactly</u>... how he thinks... Have
<u>you</u> read this file?

Batman's jaw tightens, almost imperceptibly.

                    UNSEEN PRISONER'S VOICE
You two... have so much in
<u>common</u>. Masked avengers.

But he's even more <u>righteous</u>.
Are you afraid he makes you
look <u>soft</u>?

                    BATMAN
          <u>You're wasting my time</u>—

Batman takes the file—the Prisoner CACKLES, <u>LAUGHTER
BUILDING MANIACALLY</u> as Batman rises, pressing a
BUZZER—WE PUSH IN ON THE GLASS toward the OUT-OF-
FOCUS PRISONER, head in his hands, <u>as he fights to regain
composure</u>—

               UNSEEN PRISONER'S VOICE
          OK... OK... I'll... I'll tell you what I
          <u>really</u> think...

As the CAMERA STOPS, SUPER-TIGHT on the wired glass, the
BLURRED PRISONER finally lifts his head... As he presses HIS
LIPS close to the window—<u>THEY COME INTO FOCUS—HIS
MOUTH IS DISEASED, HORRIBLY DISTORTED INTO A
RICTUS GRIN</u>—THE PRISONER IS **THE JOKER**—

Batman faces the door, waiting for it to unlock—as The Joker
continues, quiet, sadistic pleasure in his voice—

                    THE JOKER
          <u>I</u> think you don't really <u>care</u>
          about his motives, whether he
          <u>loves</u> you or <u>hates</u> you... I think...
          somewhere <u>deep down</u>... you're
          just... terrified. <u>Because you're
          not sure he's wrong</u>...

ON BATMAN—as the door suddenly UNLOCKS—hesitating—

THE JOKER
You think they <u>deserved it</u>.
Don't you...?

He opens the door—AN UNNERVINGLY LOUD BUZZING
PIERCES THE AIR as he steps out—and the DOOR SLAMS
SHUT—

SMASH TO:

SUPER-TIGHT ON BLINKING EYES—AS CONTACT LENSES GO IN—

SELINA (OS)
<u>Ow</u>—I don't know about these—

BATMAN (OS)
I need to <u>see</u> in there—seems
like this is his hunting ground—

**EXT. WAREHOUSE ROOF—ACROSS FROM ICEBERG LOUNGE—
NIGHT**

Selina turns to Batman—who's absorbed in setting up
PORTABLE SURVEILLANCE EQUIPMENT—a man on a
mission—

SELINA
Why am I starting to feel like a
fish on a hook? I'm just lookin'
for <u>Annika</u>—

(watching him work)
Boy, you're a real sweetheart—
you don't care <u>what</u> happens to
me in there tonight, do you?

No response—she looks away, when finally he turns to her—
something significant in his voice as it quiets—

                    BATMAN
              <u>Look at me</u>...

Surprised, she does—they stare into each others eyes—his
intensely studying hers, as she gazes back for a long time—
something very intimate in the moment—<u>when</u>—

                    BATMAN
              K. Looks good.

He offers her a TINY EARPIECE; she glares, snatching it—

INT. ICEBERG LOUNGE—CLOSE ON SELINA—MOVING—NIGHT

HOLD ON HER FACE as she STRIDES through the PACKED
CLUB—INTENSITY IN HER EYES as DANCE MUSIC BLASTS—

**HER CONTACT LENS POV—ON BATMAN'S LAPTOP—
SIMULTANEOUS**

PLUNGING through CHAOS—the IMAGE and SOUND
STUTTERING—AS **BATMAN** works to get a lock on her
signal—

CLOSE ON SELINA—MOVING—SIMULTANEOUS

As she HEADS into a DARKER SPACE, the MUSIC NOW
MUFFLED—

HER CONTACT LENS POV—ON BATMAN'S LAPTOP—
SIMULTANEOUS

The **SIGNAL STABILIZES**—we see she is PASSING
SHOWGIRLS AT DRESSING MIRRORS—SOME LOOK RIGHT
AT US as we pass—

> BATMAN
>
> Got you. Can you hear me?

> SELINA
> (low, not thrilled)
> Yeah—

BATMAN STARES AS SHE MOVES TO PENGUIN'S BACKROOM AREA—<u>PENGUIN LOOKS UP AT US, CONCERNED</u>—AS SELINA ARRIVES—

<u>NOTE: THESE THREE PERSPECTIVES INTERCUT THROUGHOUT THE FOLLOWING CLUB SEQUENCE—CLOSE ON SELINA ACTUALLY IN THE CLUB—HER POV ON THE LAPTOP—AND BATMAN WATCHING</u>:

> PENGUIN (ON LAPTOP)
> What's up, doll? You look tense...

> SELINA (ON SELINA)
> I wanna work downstairs tonight.

> PENGUIN (ON LAPTOP)
> (quiets, struck)
> ...downstairs? Naw, naw, you don't wanna do that—

> SELINA (ON SELINA)
> —I need the money—

> PENGUIN (ON LAPTOP)
> —baby, it's a bunch of <u>jackals</u> down there—they'll be all over you—

> SELINA (OS)
> —I'll be fine—

> PENGUIN (ON LAPTOP)
> —I'm telling you—it'd drive me
> <u>crazy</u>—
>
> (taking out wallet)
> —look—whattaya need?

> SELINA (ON SELINA)
> —Oz—

> PENGUIN (ON LAPTOP)
> —I don't <u>mind</u>—I'd do <u>anything</u>
> for you, honey—don't you know
> how I <u>feel</u> about you by now—?

> SELINA
> —<u>OZ</u>—!

He looks at her, silent, a flash of vulnerability—

> SELINA (ON SELINA)
> ...I don't want your money.

> PENGUIN (ON LAPTOP)
> (darkens, nerve hit)
> ...what? Not good enough for
> you?

She says nothing. He pulls out A KEYCARD, just holds it out, cold—as she reaches, he pulls it back—BATMAN WATCHES Penguin glare into HER POV, simmering; then—

> PENGUIN (ON LAPTOP)
> I know you don't see it yet,
> honey, nobody does... but
> Falcone ain't gonna be around
> forever. <u>One day this city's</u>
> <u>gonna be mine</u>...

She just looks at him; finally, he hands her the KEY—

POV ON THE MOVE AGAIN—BATMAN'S LAPTOP—MOMENTS LATER

BATMAN watches the POV APPROACH the MUSTACHED BOUNCER—ominously guarding an ELEVATOR—his face now bruised from their earlier fight—SELINA holds up her KEYCARD—

> SELINA
> Hospitality.

He suspiciously searches her eyes—she averts—he opens the elevator—she steps in—the doors shut—

> SELINA
> You sure no one can see these
> things in my eyes?

> BATMAN
> Don't worry. I'm watching you.

She takes a tense breath—somehow not reassured by that idea—and as the doors open—she steps—

INTO THE 44 BELOW

—another world down here; a crowded, speak-easy vibe—
SELINA SEES A LINE OF MEN all turning to size her up—
Batman sees HER POV DROP QUICKLY off their faces—

> BATMAN
> Don't look away—I need time to
> make I.D.s—

> SELINA
> (ugh)
> Great.

As she turns back, Batman sees FACIAL RECOG SCANS
BEGIN—when he NOTICES the SEA OF MEN GAZING lewdly
at her body.

> BATMAN
> These guys have a little trouble
> with eye contact, don't they?

> SELINA
> Feels nice, doesn't it?

—I.D.s start coming through on the laptop—

> BATMAN
> Guy up ahead's a city
> councilman—

> SELINA
> Guy he's talking to isn't—

> BATMAN
> No, he's not.

> (then, another I.D.)
> There's the chairman of Gotham
> First National—

> SELINA
> What'd I tellya? The <u>best</u> people.

She passes a LOUNGE AREA where THREE MEN IN SUITS sit
with TWO "HOSPITALITY GIRLS"—they're all getting high,
EYE-DROPPERS over their eyes to administer "drops"—

> SELINA
> Jesus—I hate drop heads—

> BATMAN
> Really? 'Coz when I first saw
> you, looked like you were
> dealing for Penguin—

> SELINA

—you don't know what you're
talking about—can we—can we
not do this now—?

ONE OF THE MEN turns, mid-drop, THUNDERSTRUCK
by Selina—recognizing the look, she quickly turns away
from him—

> BATMAN

Wait. Who was that—?

> SELINA

Oh, I saw him—

> BATMAN

Look back—

> SELINA

If I look back, it's gonna be a
whole can a worms—

> BATMAN

I need to see his face—

She turns back and he's still staring; he stumbles over—

> SELINA

Oh God, happy? Here he comes.

> MAN

Hey—

> BATMAN

That's the DA. Gil Colson. Talk to
him.

MAN/GIL COLSON
How you doin'? I'm Gil.

SELINA
(smiles)
Aren't you the D.A.—?

GIL COLSON
—yeah—!

SELINA
—wow—I seen you on TV!

GIL COLSON
Haven't seen <u>you</u> here before.
Helluva time to be the new girl.

People are all a little on edge.

SELINA
Honey, I live on the edge—

GIL COLSON
Oh! I like that! You wanna join
us? C'mon—

He gestures to his table—leads her over to the group—the
vibe here is a little tense—

GIL COLSON
This is Ritchie, Travis, Glen—
and you know Carla, here?

BATMAN
That's half the D.A.'s office—

Gil points to the other Hospitality Girl, who has a CATATONIC SMILE, and a dropper in hand—

> GIL COLSON
> That's Cheri—don't mind her. She's taking a break. We're just drowning our sorrows. Wanna drop?

> SELINA
> No, I'm good—but honey, you enjoy—

> GIL COLSON
> I hope you don't mind—I got a lotta weight on my shoulders with that psycho running around—

Batman sees his RED EYES—he's VERY HIGH, DISTRAUGHT—

> BATMAN
> He's wasted—

> SELINA
> No shit—

Gil looks at her, thinks she was responding to him—

> GIL COLSON
> Right? I like this girl!

> SELINA
> (recovering smoothly)
> I like you too—

She touches his hand—he looks down, disarmed, suddenly vulnerable—

> **GIL COLSON**
> I mean, you don't understand—
> this Riddler's going after the
> most powerful guys in the
> city—and he knows so <u>much</u>—

> **TRAVIS**
> He doesn't know shit, man—

> **GIL COLSON**
> He does! What about all that
> creepy shit in the video about
> the <u>rat</u>—?!

> **RITCHIE**
> Hey, c'mon, Gil—I think maybe
> you had a little too much—slow
> down—

> **BATMAN**
> <u>Wait</u>. The rat, ask about the
> rat—

> **SELINA**
> What do you mean <u>a rat</u>...?

> **GIL COLSON**
> (turns to her, intimate, hushed)
> I mean there was a rat—we had
> an <u>informant</u>! We had <u>big-time
> information on Salvatore
> Maroni</u>!

That's how we got that bastard outta the <u>drops business</u>! But if this guy <u>knows</u>, and it ever comes out <u>who the rat is, the whole city'll come APART</u>—!

CARLA

<u>Hey</u>! I don't wanna <u>hear</u> this, this is the kind of pillow talk that got that Russian girl <u>disappeared</u>!

SELINA
(turns, struck)
What? What do you know about that?

CARLA
(curt, stands up)
Anybody want a drink?

And she's gone—Selina watches her cross to THE BAR—

BATMAN
<u>Keep him talking</u>—

When Selina abruptly stands—starts off after Carla—

BATMAN
Where you going—?

SELINA
<u>She knows Annika</u>—

BATMAN
No—<u>stay on the D.A.</u>—

                              SELINA
                    —I'm lookin' for my friend—

Selina grabs Carla's arm at the bar, speaking HUSHED—

                              SELINA
                    Hey—where's Annika?

                              CARLA
                    Outta my face! I don't know
                    you—

                              SELINA
                    But you know her—who took
                    her—what have you heard—is
                    she OK?

                              CARLA
                    Jesus—keep your voice down—
                    whattaya got a death wish—?

                    AN OMINOUS MALE VOICE (OS)
                    What's the problem, ladies...?

Carla suddenly falls silent... as SELINA TURNS... BATMAN
SEES a SILHOUETTED FIGURE staring back, PENGUIN beside
him—the FACIAL SCAN struggles to I.D. the DARK FACE—

                           CARLA (OS)
                    Oh, there's no—no problem.
                    Just... girl talk. We're good.

                             PENGUIN
                    Well let's keep it festive down
                    here, OK?

Batman stares as the MAN moves into the light—he's in his 60s, STRIKING FACE—it's clear Batman knows him—the Man's face lights up as he approaches Selina—

> STRIKING MAN
>
> Hey...

> SELINA
> (voice quieting)
> ...hey.

Batman watches the way the Man looks at her(us)—

> STRIKING MAN
>
> Been a long time since I seen you down here, gorgeous. How ya been?

> SELINA (OS)
>
> Yeah, I been... OK. I was just... on my way back upstairs...

Batman stares as the Man smiles at us, a bit suggestive—

> STRIKING MAN
>
> Well don't be a stranger...

EXT. WAREHOUSE ROOF—BATMAN'S LAPTOP—MOMENTS LATER

Batman watches as Selina ENTERS A BATHROOM—stops at a sink, staring down; Batman can't see her, just the sink—

> BATMAN
>
> You know Carmine Falcone—?

SELINA (OS)
I told you—it's a <u>mob spot</u>—

BATMAN
You didn't tell me you had a
<u>relationship</u> with him—

SELINA
<u>We don't have a relationship,
OK?</u>

She glares up at her reflection, <u>removing the contacts</u>—

BATMAN
That's not how it looked—wait—
what're you doing—?

SELINA
Listen, I can't—I can't do this no
more—

And as the lenses come out—<u>HIS LAPTOP GOES BLACK—</u>
<u>HOLD ON BATMAN—INTENSE—REELING—THEN—</u>

EXT. FRONT OF ICEBERG LOUNGE—UNKNOWN POV—NIGHT

WE WATCH THROUGH FOGGED **WINDOWS OF A
PARKED SUV** as **SELINA BURSTS OUT** THE CLUB into the
FLICKERING LIGHT OF THE LONE STREETLAMP, looks for a
cab... <u>when, we hear **BREATHING**</u>... <u>AN OLIVE GREEN HOOD</u>
<u>EDGES INTO FRAME—THE BREATHING QUIETS as GIL</u>
<u>STUMBLES out of the club too</u>—

ON THE STREET

Gil calls after Selina—still smitten—still high—

> GIL COLSON
> Hey! <u>Lost</u> you in there—

> SELINA
> Yeah—I gotta go—

> GIL COLSON
> ...oh—you—need a <u>ride</u>...?

BACK INSIDE THE SUV

> GIL COLSON
> (gesturing at us)
> —that's me right <u>there</u>—

<u>HE'S POINTING RIGHT AT WHERE THE KILLER IS HIDING</u>—
<u>THE HOOD SLIPS FROM VIEW AGAIN</u>—as SELINA
GLANCES AT US—distractedly considering for an instant—
then—

> SELINA
> No—I'm—I'm good—

A GYPSY CAB thankfully arrives—she grabs the handle—

> GIL COLSON
> Well I hope I—? See you <u>round</u>?

She jumps in—slamming the door as the CAB SPEEDS OFF—

Gil watches her go, depressed... <u>the HOOD edges back into
frame, watching</u>... Gil looks to the club, considers going in...
but turns, starting in our direction—<u>as the HOOD
disappears</u>—Gil looks right at us, taking out his FOB—

OVERHEAD ON THE STREET—LOOKING STRAIGHT DOWN

—as Gil's lonely figure approaches the waiting SUV—

THROUGH THE PARTIALLY FOGGED WINDSHIELD

—we SEE Gil get in... HOLD, as he fumbles for his seatbelt—
unaware of—THE HOODED FORM SLOWLY RISING
BEHIND HIM—Gil leans forward—briefly out of its reach—
as he strains to wipe fog from the windshield—

THE KILLER REMAINS EERILY STILL—as Gil SETTLES
BACK—further than expected... He feels blindly behind to
FIND THE HEADREST GONE—confused, he turns—
SUDDENLY FACE TO HOOD WITH THE KILLER—BEFORE
HE CAN REACT—*THE KILLER PUMMELS GIL WITH HIS
METAL TOOL*—GIL SLUMPS onto the wheel—HORN
BLARING—the KILLER YANKS HIM BACK—

TIGHT ON GIL IN THE SUV

—totally out of it—BLOOD FANNING down his face—we hear
the KILLER BREATHING HARD—then the SOUND OF DUCT
TAPE RIPPING—TAPE COVERS GIL'S MOUTH—AS GIL
STARTS TO COME TO—MOANING IN PANIC—THE KILLER
LIFTS **A CRUDELY MADE CLAMP**—Gil feels it **SLIDING
AROUND HIS NECK**—HIS MOANING INTENSIFIES—HE
BEGINS TO FLAIL—

THE KILLER'S HOOD UNDULATES with <u>EACH BREATH</u>—
<u>THE AVIATOR GLASSES OVER HIS HOOD RHYTHMICALLY</u>
<u>FOGGING</u>—

> RIDDLER
> Just... hold... <u>still</u>...

We hear the **SICKENING CLICKS OF METAL CINCHING**
TIGHTER—**TIGHTER**—GIL'S <u>MOANING TURNS TO UTTER</u>
<u>TERROR</u>—AS WE—

EXT. ABANDONED SKYSCRAPER CONSTRUCTION SITE—
PRE-DAWN

A CRUISER pulls past an OLD SIGN: "**A GOTHAM**
RENEWAL PROJECT—FOR A BRIGHTER TOMORROW."
<u>GORDON gets out</u>—

ON GORDON—RISING IN A CONSTRUCTION ELEVATOR—
PRE-DAWN

As it stops, he emerges onto—

AN UNFINISHED FLOOR—HIGH ABOVE THE CITY

—walking cautiously through a maze of girders to... <u>THE</u>
<u>RUSTED BAT-SIGNAL</u>, BEAM BLAZING into the sky. He shuts
it off, thrusting the space further into darkness...

> BATMAN (OS)
> What do you know about a
> confidential informant in the
> Maroni case...?

Gordon turns, finally spotting BATMAN'S SILHOUETTE; then:

                    GORDON
Yeah, sure—there <u>was</u>...

                    BATMAN
<u>That's the rat we're looking for.</u>
Somehow Riddler knows who he
is—we find the rat, maybe that'll
lead us to <u>him</u>.

                    GORDON
Where you getting this?

                    BATMAN
I have a source who spoke to the
D.A. tonight. Gil's very nervous.

He thinks the killer's targeting
people connected to the case.

                    GORDON
...<u>I</u> worked that case too...!

                    BATMAN
Riddler's not after you—

                    GORDON
How do you know—?

                    BATMAN
You're not corrupt.

                    GORDON
...Colson's dirty?

Batman nods. Gordon shakes his head—outrage building—

> **GORDON**
> Well maybe I go <u>after</u> him—<u>lean on him</u> to give up the rat—

> **BATMAN**
> Too dangerous. Colson said they made a secret deal with this guy—whatever it is, it's huge. And who knows how many people it touches—politicians, police, the courts—it could tear the city apart.

Gordon reels—

> **GORDON**
> Jesus—this is a powder keg.

> **BATMAN**
> And Riddler's the match.

INT. "THE CAVE"—UNDERNEATH WAYNE TOWER—EARLY MORNING

VOICES ECHO as we **PAN THROUGH THE SPACE**— sweeping past the BLACK MUSCLE KIT CAR, almost complete now...

> **BATMAN (VO)**
> You know <u>Carmine Falcone</u>—?

> **SELINA (VO)**
> I told you—this is a <u>mob spot</u>—

> **BATMAN (VO)**
> You didn't tell me you had a <u>relationship</u> with him—

SELINA (VO)
<u>We don't have a relationship,</u>
<u>OK</u>?!

We FIND BRUCE at his work bench in A DARK SUIT,
examining FOOTAGE from last night—<u>FREEZING on</u>
<u>SELINA'S FACE</u>—

ALFRED (OS)
Pretty. New friend of yours?

BRUCE
I'm not so sure...

ALFRED
Looks like you upset her.

Bruce turns, annoyed—Alfred smiles—

ALFRED
Shall I take this as a good sign?

BRUCE
What?

ALFRED
Your attire. Is Bruce Wayne
making an actual appearance?

BRUCE
There's a public memorial for
Mayor Mitchell. Serial killers
like to follow reaction to their
crimes—Riddler might not be
able to resist.

                    ALFRED
          Oh, that reminds me—I took the
          liberty of doing a little work on
          this latest cipher...

Bruce looks—Alfred has decoded the SYMBOLS FROM
INSIDE THE RAT'S MAZE that was on COMMISSIONER
SAVAGE'S head—

                    ALFRED
          I'm afraid his Spanish is less
          than perfect, but I'm fairly
          certain it translates to "You are
          el rata alada"...

                    BRUCE
          "Rata alada"... rat with wings?

                    ALFRED
          It's slang for pigeon—make any
          sense to you?

                    BRUCE
          Yeah... a stool pigeon—

                    ALFRED
          —where are your cufflinks?

                    BRUCE
          Couldn't find them—

                    ALFRED
          You can't go out like that!

Bruce turns briefly to see Alfred removing his own—

                    BRUCE
          Alfred, I don't want your—

                   ALFRED
          You have to keep up
          appearances—you're still a
          Wayne—

Annoyed, Bruce relents, letting Alfred slip one on—he sees a
MONOGRAMMED **W** on the link—gives Alfred a look—

                    BRUCE
          What about you? Are you a
          Wayne?

                   ALFRED
             (doing other sleeve)
          Your father gave them to me...

That catches Bruce off guard—he looks at him, thrown—when
Alfred glances up with a smile, making light—

                   ALFRED
          I'm just loaning them to you—I
          want them back...

And as Bruce nods, a DIN OF HORNS AND TRAFFIC
SWELLS—

INT. BRUCE'S VINTAGE SPORTS CAR—DAY

CLOSE ON THE **W** CUFFLINK as Bruce drives—approaching
CITY HALL—he gazes at the street PACKED WITH
MOURNERS, MAKESHIFT MEMORIALS... his blood chills
as he SEES—

AN OLIVE HOODED MAN in the crowd with a sign—a **SCRAWLED QUESTION MARK IN CROSSHAIRS**—not far behind, ANOTHER HOODED MAN holds one that says: **WHO ELSE DIES FOR GOTHAM'S LIES?** ANOTHER holds: **OUR DAY OF JUDGEMENT**—

Bruce stares at the RIDDLER-INSPIRED PROTESTORS—when a TRAFFIC COP presses to the window, double-takes, seeing Bruce. Bruce strains a smile—as the Cop waves him in—

EXT. FRONT OF GOTHAM CITY HALL—DAY

Bruce gets out as a VALET opens his door—when—

> PAPARAZZO (OS)
> ...is that Bruce Wayne...?

Heads turn—as news spreads—CAMERAS BEGIN FLASHING—

> PAPARAZZI
> ...Mr. Wayne?! Mr. Wayne!

Bruce ignores them, reaching for his wallet as he hears—

> A VOICE (OS)
> —can I helpya, Mr. Falcone?

Bruce spins to see BODYGUARDS helping Carmine Falcone out of a car—Falcone turns as a WOMAN climbs out in a HIGH-SLIT DRESS—REMINISCENT OF SELINA'S—her **FACE IS CONCEALED** under a VEILED HAT—she takes Falcone's hand as they join his PHALANX OF GUARDS—Bruce's eyes track her: is that Selina? He hands the Valet a wad of cash—

BRUCE

Keep it close—

Bruce moves after her—through the thick crowd, bottle-
necking by the entrance—eyes on the Woman—pressing into
FALCONE'S SECURITY TEAM, <u>trying to glimpse her veiled
face</u>—when <u>A HAND slaps into his chest</u>—

PENGUIN

Hey—<u>hey</u>—give us a wide berth
here—<u>willya</u>, slick?!

Bodyguards grab Bruce too—hearing the commotion, the
Woman turns—Bruce SEES—<u>it's CARLA</u>—

FALCONE

Watchit, fellas—you got the
prince of the city there!

They loosen their grip as Falcone steps over, smiles—

> FALCONE
> Some event, brought out the one
> guy in the city more reclusive
> than <u>me</u>.

Bruce glares with edge, a sense of history between them—

> BRUCE
> I thought you never leave the
> Shoreline—aren't you afraid
> someone'll take a shot at you?

> FALCONE
> Ya mean now that your <u>father</u>
> ain't around? Oz, you know
> Bruce Wayne?

> PENGUIN
> Whoa—<u>seriously</u>?!

> FALCONE
> His father saved my life. I got
> shot in the chest, <u>right here</u>.
>
> Couldn't go to no hospital, so we
> showed up on his doorstep. He
> took me in, operated right on his
> dining room table—kid here saw
> the whole thing.
>
> (to Bruce)
> You don't think that <u>meant</u>
> something, he did that?

> BRUCE
> Means he took the Hippocratic
> Oath.

> FALCONE
> ...Hippocratic Oath, right... that's
> good...

> BRUCE
> —s'cuse me—

And Bruce abruptly moves on, the bottleneck opening—

INT. GOTHAM CITY HALL—MOVING WITH BRUCE—DAY

A SEXTET PLAYS as MOURNERS continue to flood in—on the
prowl, BRUCE SCANS the crowd—he CLOCKS RIFLED
OFFICERS among SPECTATORS above—studies the CRUSH
OF FACES in the STANDING PUBLIC GALLERY—some back
here in tears—

> P.A. ANNOUNCER
> Ladies and gentlemen, thank
> you all for coming to today's
> memorial for our beloved
> mayor, Don Mitchell, Jr. Our
> program will begin shortly. As
> a reminder, the family asks
> that those wishing to honor
> the mayor's memory consider
> a donation to the cause most
> dear to his heart, the Gotham
> Renewal Fund, our city's
> safety net.

—Bruce sees COPS STOPPING a SUSPICIOUS GUY—when—

                    AN EERIE VOICE BEHIND (OS)
                    What good's a safety net doesn't
                    <u>catch</u> anybody...?

Bruce turns—to see A BITTER NOBODY in a hooded work
jacket, angry eyes on the VIPS as they file past—

                    BITTER NOBODY
                    Didn't help <u>my</u> daughter when
                    she needed it—I can tell you <u>that</u>.
                    Guy was just another <u>rich
                    scum</u>sucker. He got what he
                    deserved.

Finally, his eyes shift to Bruce, <u>a truly chilling look</u>—

                    BITTER NOBODY
                    <u>Yeah, I said it</u>...

Bruce studies his acne-scarred face—nodding—when—the
man's expression changes—trying to place Bruce—

                    BITTER NOBODY
                    ...hey... don't I <u>know</u> you?

                    A WOMAN'S VOICE
                    <u>Bruce Wayne</u>—

Startled, Bruce spins to see BELLA REÁL coming at him—

                    BELLA REÁL
                    <u>Why haven't you called me
                    back</u>?

BRUCE

...I'm sorry—?

BELLA REÁL

(no-nonsense)

I'm Bella Reál—I'm running for
mayor—I wouldn't be bothering
you here, but your people keep
telling me you're "unavailable".
<u>Will you walk with me</u>?

On the spot, Bruce glances back at the man—who now
<u>glowers</u>—Bella tucks her arm under Bruce's—stealing him—
he sneaks a look at the BITTER NOBODY who glares as they
recede—then turns, <u>disappearing in the crowd</u>—

She leads Bruce to THE SEATED AREA, quiets, still blunt:

BELLA REÁL

You know you really could
be doing more for the city—
your family has a history of
philanthropy, but as far as I can
tell, you're not doing anything—
if I'm elected, I wanna change
that—

She smiles disarmingly as they near the front—a BOY'S
CHOIR on the central steps begins <u>SHUBERT'S "**AVE
MARIA**"</u>—

BELLA REÁL

Will you wait for me? I wanna go
pay my respects—my God, what
a mess—his poor wife and son...

And she leaves him; struck by her nerve and charisma, Bruce watches her lean into the row to greet the widow—when the Mayor's Ten-Year-Old Son glances awkwardly back—making brief eye contact—a sad moment—when—

> HUSHED, FAMILIAR VOICE (OS)
> 'Scuse me, Chief? Can I talk to
> you...?

Bruce turns to spy GORDON with OFFICERS, a few rows back—Gordon touches the arm of the seated CHIEF OF POLICE—

> GORDON
> Gil Colson is missing...

> CHIEF BOCK
> ...what?

> GORDON
> He hasn't been heard from since
> last night—

—when one of the Officers, Martinez, suddenly notices Bruce gazing in their direction—a surprised smile—

> MARTINEZ
> ...hey, Mr. Wayne...

Gordon falls silent—a strange moment for Bruce as Batman's closest ally glares warily at the billionaire—

TIGHT ON BRUCE as he turns away—still listening—

> CHIEF BOCK (OS)
> Christ, not again—you got
> people looking for him, Jim?

WHEN SUDDENLY—DISTANT SCREAMS—an AWFUL
GROANING ENGINE WHINES from somewhere outside—
then—SICKENING THUDS—BRUCE'S EYES IMMEDIATELY
FLIT UP IN ALARM TO—

THE SECOND STORY LANDING where SPECTATORS
PANIC—<u>SEEING SOMETHING THROUGH THE WINDOWS</u>—
EVERYONE TURNING—ALL EXCEPT **A SILHOUETTED
FIGURE**—GAZING EERILY DOWN IN BRUCE'S DIRECTION—
<u>WAITING FOR SOMETHING</u>—WHEN—

<u>**BAMMMMMM!!!**</u> <u>THE MAIN ENTRANCE EXPLODES IN
A BLIZZARD OF GLASS AND CONCRETE</u>—**AS THE D.A.'S
SUV RIPS THROUGH THE DOORS**—<u>FLOWERS PICKED
UP IN THE GRILL</u>—**PANDEMONIUM**—AS THE CROWD
SCATTERS—SOME TOSSED INTO THE AIR—THE VEHICLE
SLAMMING PAST GUARDRAILS INTO THE SEATED AREA—

BRUCE SPINS—<u>TO SEE THE MAYOR'S SON A FEW FEET AWAY</u>—FROZEN IN SHOCK AS OTHERS FLEE ALL AROUND HIM—HE HURLS HIMSELF AT THE BOY—**TACKLING HIM OUT OF THE SUV'S PATH AS IT ROARS PAST**— LAUNCHING SEATS OVER THEIR HEADS—**FINALLY CRASHING** INTO THE CENTRAL STAIRCASE—BUCKLING UPWARD—**ENGINE GRINDING—TILL IT... <u>STOPS</u>**...

A surreal moment of quiet, then screams, tears, panic— as Bruce lifts his head off the boy's to look over at the wreck—then up AT THE SECOND FLOOR: **THE FIGURE'S <u>GONE</u>**—people flee in all directions, as BRUCE RISES— watching the boy run to his mother's arms—BRUCE TURNS TO SEE—

GORDON AND TEN COPS SURROUNDING THE SUV— GUNS RAISED—THE SUV IS COVERED IN A SCRAWLED **CROSSWORD PUZZLE PATTERN**—THE ENDLESSLY REPEATING MESSAGE: "**D.A.—D.O.A.?**"

BRUCE edges closer past FLEEING MOURNERS—WHEN— THE DENTED DRIVER DOOR SUDDENLY **<u>CRACKS OPEN</u>—<u>THE HALL RINGS WITH THE CLAMOR OF DOZENS OF BULLETS CHAMBERED AT ONCE</u>**—

> GORDON
> GET OUTTA THE CAR! HANDS
> UP!

Bruce watches the driver door slowly open all the way... A FIGURE staggers out, hands raised, terrified—

> GORDON
> Holy Christ... <u>it's Colson</u>.

The D.A. has a bloody face, tape over his mouth with the words "NO MORE LIES"—the CLAMP STILL AROUND HIS NECK—**LIGHTS RAPIDLY FLASH** ON IT—a cop notices, horrified—

COP

There's a BOMB around his neck!!!

—a **BEEP-BEEP-BEEP!** RINGS OUT—EVERYONE FREAKS— SHIELDING THEMSELVES—except Bruce who just stares at— the D.A. who REMAINS IN ONE PIECE—everyone looks up, confused... when the D.A.—sheepishly lifts his hand... Pointing to A CELL TAPED TO HIS PALM—as BEEP-BEEP-BEEP—it RINGS again—Gordon turns, calling to the room—

GORDON

Let's get this place cleared! Now!

Police begin ushering people out—but Bruce hesitates, chilled, as he notices... taped to the D.A.'s chest is A GREETING CARD; it's addressed: "**To The Batman**"...

BLACKNESS LIFTS

REVEALING BRUCE as he leans in, REACHING INTO THE TRUNK OF HIS CAR—SEIZING AN EXPENSIVE **LEATHER DUFFLE**—

WIDE SHOT—OUTSIDE GOTHAM CITY HALL—CONTINUOUS

Bruce slams his trunk—disappearing into the crowd—as a FLOOD OF EMERGENCY VEHICLES SCREECH INTO VIEW—

EXT. GOTHAM CITY HALL—SHORT TIME LATER

Jammed with POLICE, SWAT, ATF, K9 UNITS, NEWS
CREWS—outside a **CRISIS COMMAND TRAILER**, TECHS
set up MONITORS as THE LEADS ARGUE—GORDON and
HIS MEN watch, appalled:

> GORDON
> ...<u>un</u>believable...

> MARTINEZ
> They're fightin' over
> <u>jurisdiction</u>, and that poor
> bastard's gonna <u>blow</u>...!

INSIDE THE EVACUATED CITY HALL

A SWAT TEAM crouches behind BLAST SHIELDS in the
doorway, <u>RIFLES TRAINED ON GIL, sitting alone in the</u>
<u>distance</u>—the cell on his hand echoing as it <u>JUST KEEPS</u>
<u>RINGING</u>... GIL lifts his head, hopeless, as a SMALL,
WHIRRING POLICE ROBOT rolls to a stop before him. He
stares oddly as a camera slowly extends toward his head—

CRISIS COMMAND—CONTINUOUS

A COMMAND CRISIS TECH at ONE OF THE MONITORS yells
out—

> COMMAND CRISIS TECH
> <u>We got a picture!</u>

The Leads suddenly quiet—crowding around to see—GIL
STARING SADLY INTO THE ROBOT CAMERA—when
suddenly he turns, struck—shock beginning to fill his eyes—

CHIEF BOCK
...what's he lookin' at...?

INSIDE CITY HALL

Gil sits there, frozen—as—**BATMAN EMERGES FROM THE SHADOWS**—moving slowly across the floor toward him—

SWAT TEAM MEMBER
...holy shit...

CHIEF BOCK'S EYES WIDEN

As Batman appears on the ROBOT'S CAMERAS—

CHIEF BOCK
...are you kiddin' me?! What the
hell's he doin'...?! Gordon!!!

Gordon presses closer to see BATMAN APPROACHING GIL—

CHIEF BOCK
Your guy's gonna get himself
killed in there...!

Gordon watches, with growing concern—AS—

INSIDE CITY HALL

Batman stops, towering over Gil—who rises, scared... Batman reaches out, peels THE TAPE OFF HIS MOUTH—

GIL COLSON
He made me do it—said if I didn't
do exactly what he said he'd kill
me—please—can't somebody get
this thing off?!

BATMAN
Looks like a combination lock—

GIL COLSON
—can't you <u>cut</u> it off...?!

Batman carefully touches a NASTY SNARL OF TRIP WIRES—

BATMAN
Not if you want to keep your
head.

Batman rips the CARD off Gil's chest—ON THE COVER is a
cartoon of an OLD PHONE LITERALLY RINGING OFF THE
HOOK: "**In These Trying Times, Never Forget...**" Batman
opens it: "**...I'm Just A Phone Call Away**"—under that, in
ANGRY SCRAWL: "**<u>ANSWER</u>**". Batman points to the RINGING
CELL—Gil lifts it—<u>as Batman reaches to PRESS ANSWER</u>—

GIL COLSON
—wait—<u>wait, NO</u>—<u>WHAT IF
IT'S CONNECTED TO THE</u>—?

"<u>**BONNNG!**</u>"—the **PHONE'S SCREEN DISPLAYS A LIVE
SPLIT-SCREEN IMAGE: RIDDLER ON ONE SIDE,
BATMAN AND GIL ON THE OTHER**—Riddler stares from
under his hood for a beat... then **HIS CHILLING VOICE
COMES CALMLY THROUGH THE CHANGER:**

RIDDLER
...you <u>came</u>...

BATMAN
...<u>who are you</u>?

                    RIDDLER
Me? I'm... I'm nobody. I'm just...
an <u>instrument</u>... Here to unmask
the <u>truth</u> about this <u>cesspool</u>...
we call a city...

                    BATMAN
...unmask...?

                    RIDDLER
Yes... let's do it together, OK?
I've been trying to reach you...
<u>You're</u> part of this too...

                    BATMAN
<u>Me</u>? How am <u>I</u> part of this?

                    RIDDLER
    <u>You'll</u> see...

CRISIS COMMAND—CONTINUOUS

Everyone presses around another MONITOR in horror—<u>GC1</u>
<u>running the FEED FROM RIDDLER'S PHONE,</u> broadcasting
live through social media—"**<u>BATMAN TALKS TO KILLER</u>**
<u>LIVE</u>"

                    RIDDLER (ON MONITOR)
            Say hello to my <u>followers</u>—we're
            live! They're here to watch our
            little <u>trial</u>...

Bock turns to the Tech—beside himself—

                    CHIEF BOCK
            <u>Can you trace the goddamn call</u>?!

COMMAND CRISIS TECH
(throws up hands)
It's—it's not a <u>call</u>, chief—it's
an <u>app</u>—

BACK INSIDE CITY HALL

Riddler gazing back at Batman and Gil through the phone—

RIDDLER
At the moment... the man across
from you, Mr. Colson, is <u>dead</u>—

GIL COLSON
(panics)
Jesus <u>CHRIST</u>—

RIDDLER
(chilling calm)
—wait a minute—

GIL COLSON
—can we <u>PLEASE</u> get somebody
<u>OVER HERE</u>—?!

RIDDLER
—shut up—

GIL COLSON
—THIS PSYCHO'S GONNA <u>KILL</u>
ME—!

RIDDLER
(scarily distorted)
<u>SHUUUUUT UUUUUP—</u>

RIDDLER

**—you DESERVE to be dead
after what you did!!! You HEAR
ME?!!!**

THE TERRIFYING OUTBURST MAKES GIL FALL SILENT—

RIDDLER
(then, oddly calm)
I'm giving you a <u>chance</u>. No
one... ever... gave <u>me</u> a chance...

(then)
Now... ever since I was a child,
I've always loved little puzzles...
For me, they're... a <u>retreat</u> from
the horrors of our world...
Maybe they can bring some
comfort to <u>you too</u>, Mr. Colson.

GIL COLSON
You... want me to do... <u>puzzles</u>?

RIDDLER
Yes. Three riddles. In two
minutes. You give me the
answers, and <u>I'll give you the
code for the lock</u>. Do... you...
understand...?

GIL COLSON
—uh—OK, yeah—so you just—
you want me to—?

BEEP!—GIL SHRIEKS—**A COUNTDOWN APPEARS ON THE COLLAR**—**2:00 MINUTES**—and Riddler starts without warning—

> RIDDLER
>
> Riddle number ONE: It can be cruel, poetic, or blind... but when it's denied, it's violence you may find.

> GIL COLSON
>
> —w-w-wait—can you repeat that—I didn't—I didn't—cruel... poetic...?

> BATMAN
>
> Justice...

> GIL COLSON
>
> ...what?

> BATMAN
>
> The answer's justice.

> RIDDLER
>
> Yes. Justice. And you... were supposed to be an arm of justice in this city, along with the late mayor and police commissioner... were you not, Mr. Prosecutor...?

> GIL COLSON
>
> Well, yeah, I mean, of course we—

RIDDLER

Riddle number TWO: If you are
justice, please do not lie, what is
the price for your blind eye?

GIL COLSON

...price...?

BATMAN

Bribes.

GIL COLSON

...oh God—

BATMAN

—he's asking how much it
costs... for you to turn your
back—

GIL COLSON

—ya gotta be kiddin' me—

BATMAN

—how much—?

GIL COLSON

—like I'm the only one?? I didn't
do anything worse than anyone
else!

RIDDLER

—fifty-eight seconds...!

BATMAN

—how MUCH—?

Gil hesitates... can't <u>believe</u> he's doing this... then...

> **GIL COLSON**
> ...ten... grand. Ten Gs a month. I take a... monthly payment not to prosecute... certain cases...

> **BATMAN**
> <u>What</u> cases?

> **GIL COLSON**
> <u>Hey</u>, he didn't <u>ask</u> that—c'mon—ten grand—<u>that's your answer</u>!

> **RIDDLER**
> OK, OK, don't <u>lose your HEAD, Mr. Colson</u>! Just one more to go... before your time... runs... out. <u>Last riddle</u>: Since your justice is <u>so select</u>, please tell us which <u>vermin</u> you're paid to protect...

> **GIL COLSON**
> Jesus... which <u>vermin</u>...?

> **BATMAN**
> The <u>rat</u>. The informant you all protect...

> **GIL COLSON**
> ...how do <u>you</u> know about that—?

> **BATMAN**
> —I'm trying to <u>help</u> you—what's his <u>name</u>—?

GIL COLSON

—no... no-no-no-no-no—you
don't understand—

RIDDLER

—twenty seconds—!

BATMAN

(grabbing him hard)
—he's gonna kill you—!

GIL COLSON

—I'm dead either way! You're
talking to a DEAD MAN, OK? If I
go THIS way it's just ME—but I
give you that NAME—I got
FAMILY—people I CARE
about—they'll KILL THEM
TOO—!

BATMAN

—what are you talking about—?

GIL COLSON

—people are WATCHING—

BATMAN

—what people—WHO—?

GIL COLSON

LISTEN TO ME, GODDAMMIT—
YOU MAY **THINK** YOU KNOW
WHAT THIS IS, BUT YOU
DON'T—IT'S **SO MUCH
BIGGER** THAN YOU COULD

EVER IMAGINE, **IT'S THE
WHOLE SYSTEM**—

RIDDLER
Five...!   Four...!   Three...!

RIDDLER
—**GOOD byyyyyyyyye**—

GIL COLSON
—OH NO—OH GOD—
SOMEBODY GET THIS OFFA
ME—SOMEBODY GET THIS—

TIGHT ON BATMAN—SEEING THE COUNTER HIT **00:00**—
HE TURNS—SHIELDING HIMSELF—AS KA-**BOOOOOOOM!**—
**AT LAST ERUPTS—PROPELLING BATMAN BACK—BAT
SUIT IN FLAMES—AS HE SLAMS TO THE FLOOR**—
SMOKE SWALLOWING HIM—AND US!!! WE HEAR ONLY
HIGH-PITCHED RINGING—

BATMAN LIES—DAZED—HE STRUGGLES TO LIFT HIS
EYES—AS GORDON RUSHES FORWARD—OTHER COPS
TOO—GUNS DRAWN—SOME AROUND GIL'S NOW
LIFELESS BODY—OTHERS AROUND BATMAN—WHO
GAZES BACK, **VISION BLURRING**—COPS YELLING ALL
AROUND HIM—AS HE **BLACKS OUT**—

INT. GCPD—INTERROGATION ROOM—BATMAN'S POV—NIGHT

BATMAN COMES TO—FOCUSING on a TACTICAL MEDIC
shining light in his eyes—VOICES FADE IN—cops above in
debate, gazing down with contempt—Gordon holding them
off—when one grabs for Batman's mask—

MUSCLE COP

—what're we doin' here—just take it <u>off</u>—

GORDON

—<u>hey-hey-hey</u>—!

<u>BATMAN'S HAND SHOOTS UP, GRIPPING MUSCLE COP'S ARM</u>—<u>on the verge of violence</u>—Gordon pushes the cop back—giving Batman room to rise off the interrogation table—

CHIEF BOCK

You protecting this guy, Gordon?! He interfered in an active hostage situation! Colson's blood is on <u>his hands</u>!

BATMAN

Maybe it's on <u>yours</u>.

CHIEF BOCK

...what'd you say?!

BATMAN

He'd rather <u>die</u> than talk. What was he afraid of? <u>You</u>?

CHIEF BOCK

You sonuvabitch! You have any idea what kinda <u>trouble you're in</u>?! You could be <u>an accessory to MURDER</u>!

MUSCLE COP
Why we playin' games here,
Chief?!

He GRABS ONTO THE COWL—BATMAN ERUPTS—
KNOCKING HIM OFF BALANCE—MORE COPS LAUNCH
THEMSELVES at Batman—a WILD MELEE—Batman having
his way with them—as the room goes crazy—ALARMED,
GORDON TRIES TO BREAK IT UP—

GORDON
Whoa—back off—BACK OFF—!

CHIEF BOCK
GREAT—NOW I GOT YOU ON
<u>ASSAULTING AN OFFICER</u>!!!

> BATMAN
> (steps at cops again)
> You got me on assaulting
> three—

> GORDON
> —HEY HEY HEY—WHAT'S THE
> **MATTER** WITH YOU—?!

GORDON PUSHES HIM BACK SURPRISINGLY HARD—
BATMAN STOPS, SHOCKED, eyes flaring—Gordon glares
back, serious—their eyes locking... until Batman fills with
contempt...

> BATMAN
> ...you too now...?

> GORDON
> (dark eyes on Batman)
> Lemme handle this, Chief—
> gimme a minute...

> CHIEF BOCK
> You gonna put yourself on the
> line for this scumbag, Jim...!?

> GORDON
> Just... gimme a minute...

And he opens the door—tensely escorts Batman out—

INTO THE HALL

—as cops crowd out to watch from a distance... At the far end,
Gordon gives Batman a shove—they face each other—angry
expressions—Gordon utters, low—

GORDON
We gotta get you outta here...

Batman responds in kind, <u>making it look like an argument</u>:

BATMAN
That'll put a lotta heat on you.

GORDON
Well, you <u>punched me</u> in the
face.

BATMAN
Uh-huh—

GORDON
Those stairs lead to the roof—

Batman's eyes clock the door—when beyond it <u>he SPOTS—A</u>
<u>GROUP OF DETECTIVES</u> conferring—struck, realizing **ONE**
IS THE MUSTACHED BOUNCER FROM THE ICEBERG
LOUNGE—!

BATMAN
<u>Who's the mustache?</u>

GORDON
That's Kenzie in narcotics—

BATMAN
...<u>he's one of the guys I got into it</u>
<u>with at the Iceberg Lounge.</u>

GORDON
...what are you <u>saying</u>? Kenzie
moonlights for <u>Penguin</u>?

BATMAN
Or he moonlights as a <u>cop</u>—

When <u>KENZIE SEES BATMAN</u> staring—alarmed—<u>AND</u> <u>WITHOUT WARNING, **BATMAN PUNCHES GORDON**</u> <u>**RIGHT IN THE FACE**—GORDON GOES DOWN</u>—BATMAN <u>BREAKS FOR THE STAIRWELL</u>—<u>THE COPS STARTING</u> <u>MADLY DOWN THE HALL AFTER HIM</u>—!

IN THE STAIRWELL

BATMAN RIPS OUT HIS GRAPPLE GUN—LAUNCHING THE HOOK TO THE RAILING, TEN STORIES ABOVE— RETRACTING THE LINE—LIFTING UPWARDS—AS COPS ENTER—**FIRING AFTER HIM**—!

ON THE ROOF

BATMAN BLASTS FROM THE STAIRWELL—TO THE EDGE—GAZING AT THE HUGE DROP—THE DIN OF COPS APPROACHING—HE REACHES DOWN—YANKING **TABS** ON EACH HEEL—**ZIPPING HIS CLOAK TO HIS BOOTS**— **HIS LEGS**—**HIS ARMS**—

—THE COPS CHARGE THE ROOF—**AIMING AT BATMAN**— AS HE **PLUMMETS OFF THE EDGE**—THE COPS RACE OVER TO SEE—<u>BATMAN SOARING WILDLY DOWN</u>—**HIS CAPE** **NOW A WINGSUIT**—

THEIR SHOCKED FACES RECEDE—**AS WE FLY WITH** **BATMAN**—DESCENDING RAPIDLY, DANGEROUSLY—TO THE STREET BELOW—WHERE BATMAN HITS INTO A **HARD SHOULDER-ROLL**—**SPINNING WILDLY TO HIS** **FEET**—AND DISAPPEARING INTO THE NIGHT...

EXT. UNFINISHED SKYSCRAPER—HIGH OVER THE CITY—NIGHT

Batman waits in the RAIN... as the ELEVATOR ARRIVES...
Gordon steps out, FACE BRUISED—shaking his head—

> GORDON
>
> ...could've at least pulled your
> punch, man...

> BATMAN
>
> I <u>did</u>.

> GORDON
>
> Bock put out an A.P.B on you...
> you really think he's in on this?

> BATMAN
>
> I don't trust <u>any</u> of them, do <u>you</u>?

> GORDON
>
> I only trust <u>you</u>—

> BATMAN
>
> <u>What's a narcotics cop doing</u>
> <u>with Falcone's right-hand man</u>...?

> GORDON
>
> Colson said cops protect the rat.
> Maybe Kenzie's part of it.

> BATMAN
>
> ...you think Penguin's the rat?

> GORDON
>
> His club caters to the mob,
> Maroni was a regular—Penguin
> would've been privy to a <u>lotta</u>
> <u>dirt</u>—

And the D.A. was a regular too—maybe Penguin got himself into some trouble, and making a deal was his way out...

BATMAN
...the rata alada...

GORDON
The what?

BATMAN
Riddler's latest, that cipher in the maze. Means a rat with wings—like a stool pigeon.

GORDON
(getting it)
A penguin's got wings too.

BATMAN
Time for me to have another conversation with him—

GORDON
What about The Riddler? He's gonna kill again.

BATMAN
It's all connected—like it or not, it's his game now. We wanna find Riddler, we gotta find that rat...

GORDON
Think Penguin'll talk—?

> BATMAN
> I'll be persuasive...

EXT. ICEBERG LOUNGE—ALLEY—POV OUT WINDSHIELD—NIGHT

MENACING BREATHING as we lurk... watching the rear of the club through RAIN and FOG as WIPERS SWISH... The BREATHS STOP as PENGUIN exits with KENZIE and TWINS—Kenzie has **TWO DUFFLES**; he opens the trunk of his CAMRY—

> GORDON (OVER RADIO)
> Wonder what's in the bags...
> Should we move in...?

INT. GORDON'S CRUISER—SAME MOMENT

Gordon waits tensely with his WALKIE, watching Penguin and Twins get into an ESCALADE—when an ANSWER COMES:

> BATMAN (OVER RADIO)
> Let's follow them.

—the cars take off past Gordon—

EXT. WATERFRONT STREET—DESERTED WAREHOUSE—NIGHT

The Camry and Escalade stop by a weathered sign: **"GOTHAM RECYCLING—A RENEWAL CORP"**—Kenzie HONKS his horn—a ROLL-DOOR LIFTS—he and Penguin get out—

INT. GORDON'S CRUISER—BELOW AN UNDERPASS—SAME MOMENT

Gordon sees them approach the building; lifts his WALKIE:

> **GORDON**
> They stopped on Waterfront
> Street—the recycling plant—

—a beat—then Batman crackles quietly back—

> **BATMAN (OVER RADIO)**
> I'm here...

HIGH OVER PENGUIN AND KENZIE—FROM THE WAREHOUSE ROOF

A COWL presses into frame: BATMAN. The two men enter the building—MOVE with Batman—to LOOK IN A SKYLIGHT at the PLANT BELOW—where WORKERS lead Penguin to a CREW IN SURGICAL MASKS filling VIALS WITH CHEMICALS by BUBBLING COOKERS. Penguin inspects the operation.

A MAN IN A SUIT arrives, shaking his hand—Batman watches as **EYE-DROPPERS** are screwed onto the vials—

> **BATMAN**
> (whispers to wrist)
> It's a drug lab. Drops. This is a
> buy...

> **GORDON (OVER RADIO)**
> Looks like they got Maroni's
> operation up and running again.

> **BATMAN**
> Or they never shut it down at all.

> GORDON (OVER RADIO)
> What're you saying? Biggest
> drug bust in GCPD history was a
> <u>fraud</u>?

—Batman spots a GLINT STRAFING from below, moves to the edge—a DARK FIGURE COASTS ON A MOTORCYCLE in the alley—**SELINA IN HER CATSUIT**—she hops off, uncoiling her MOTORCYCLE LOCK CHAIN—Batman whispers into his wrist—

> BATMAN
> ...<u>this just got complicated</u>.

INT. GORDON'S CRUISER—SAME MOMENT

He cocks his head, quizzical—

> GORDON
> Whattaya mean...?

ON THE COBBLESTONES IN FRONT

The TWINS stand under umbrellas by the Camry—ONE HEARS a CLINK by his feet—looks down to see <u>THE LOCK CHAIN LOOPING FROM UNDER THE CAR AROUND HIS ANKLES—IT YANKS TIGHT—SENDING HIM FACE-FIRST INTO THE GROUND</u>—the other twin turns—confused—where'd my brother go? He moves around to see—<u>SELINA</u> **WIELDING THE CHAIN LIKE A WHIP**—<u>SNAPPING IT INTO HIS FACE—HE CRUMPLES TOO</u>—

SELINA POPS THE TRUNK—FLIPS HER VISOR, GAZING INSIDE AT A **TRIO OF DUFFLES**—UNZIPS ONE—<u>STUFFED WITH **CASH**</u>—

>   A VOICE BEHIND HER (OS)
>   Dangerous crowd you're
>   stealing from—

SELINA SPINS—READY TO STRIKE—<u>when she sees</u>
BATMAN—

>   SELINA/CATWOMAN
>   <u>Jesus</u>... this how you get your
>   kicks, hon? Sneaking up on girls
>   in the dark?

>   BATMAN
>   That why you work at the club—?
>   It was all just a <u>score</u>—?

>   SELINA/CATWOMAN
>   (back to work)
>   You know, I'd love to sit here
>   and go over every gory detail
>   with you, bat boy—but those
>   assholes'll be back—

She shoulders two duffles, unzips the third—FALLING
SILENT. Batman moves closer... <u>inside is a</u> **BODY**. Filling with
dread, she opens the bag further to see—**ANNIKA'S FACE**—
<u>Selina is rocked</u>... eyes well with rage, <u>tears</u>—

<u>WHEN SUDDENLY THE CAMRY IS RIDDLED WITH</u>
<u>GUNFIRE!</u> <u>BATMAN LUNGES FOR SELINA</u>—<u>PUSHING HER</u>
<u>TO COVER</u>—<u>AS HE TAKES ON</u> **A HAIL OF BULLETS**—
<u>SELINA SPINS</u>—<u>TO SEE</u> **BATMAN, MOTIONLESS ON THE**
GROUND—<u>SHE PEEKS OUT TO SEE</u>—

PENGUIN BY THE ROLL-DOOR—**FIRING AN UZI PISTOL**—
BACKED UP BY KENZIE AND A CREW OF THUGS—
FIRING TOO—

GORDON

HITS THE GAS—SCREECHING CLOSER—SKIDDING TO A
STOP—JUMPS BEHIND THE DRIVER DOOR—RAISING HIS
GUN—AS—

PENGUIN

STALKS FOR THE CAMRY, SHOOTING, BERSERK—KENZIE
GRABS THE DUFFLES OF MONEY—AS THE OTHERS FIRE
AT GORDON—

SELINA CRAWLS ON HANDS AND KNEES IN TERROR—SHE
LOOKS BACK TO WHERE BATMAN FELL—**BUT HE IS NO
LONGER THERE**—

SUDDENLY A GUTTERAL, TERRIFYINGLY LOUD ENGINE GROWLS! PENGUIN SPINS TO THE INKY DARKNESS OF THE ALLEY TO SEE—FLAMES SHOOTING OMINOUSLY FROM SIDE EXHAUSTS—RED NITROUS VAPOR BLASTS—THE FLASHES REVEALING A MENACING FORM—A VISION FROM A HORROR MOVIE—**THE BATMOBILE!**

PENGUIN AND THE OTHERS GAPE AT THE EMBLEM OF VENGEANCE!

AND PENGUIN JUST BOLTS FOR THE ESCALADE—DIVING IN—

KENZIE ABOUT TO FOLLOW—WHEN **A ROAR** COMES FROM THE OPPOSITE DIRECTION—**SELINA CHARGING HIM ON HER BIKE—SNATCHING THE DUFFLES RIGHT FROM HIS HAND**—**RACING AWAY**!

PENGUIN'S ESCALADE SCREECHES OUT—**THE BATMOBILE CATAPULTING AFTER HIM—WITH A CRAZY NITROUS HIT—FISHTAILING—TIRES FINALLY GRIPPING GROUND—GORDON WATCHING IN AWE AS IT VANISHES INTO THE FOG AND RAIN**—!

INT./EXT. DRIVING ON GOTHAM STREETS—IMMEDIATELY

TIRES VIOLENTLY DRUMMING ON WET COBBLESTONES— PENGUIN MANNING THE ESCALADE IN PANIC—AS— THE BATMOBILE CHARGES IN AND OUT OF VIEW LIKE A RAGING, HUNGRY SHARK—**ENGINE SHRIEKING**— **BAM-SCREEEEEE!!!**—IT SLAMS BRUTALLY INTO THE ESCALADE—TRYING TO MUSCLE IT OFF THE ROAD!!!

PENGUIN

—JESUS **CHRISTMAS**—!!!

PENGUIN SCRAMBLES FOR HIS UZI—UNLEASHING IT THROUGH HIS PASSENGER WINDOW—GLASS AND BULLETS SPRAYING THE BATMOBILE—HITS SPARKING OFF ITS ARMORED SURFACE AND BULLET-PROOF WINDOWS—AS IT SLAMS: **BAM-SCREEEEEE!!!**—HARD INTO THE ESCALADE AGAIN!

PENGUIN STRUGGLES FOR CONTROL—SUDDENLY CRANKING THE WHEEL—STEERING OFF THE ROAD— **LURCHING WILDLY UP AN MBANKMENT—RIGHT ONTO THE HIGHWAY**—!

90 MPH TRAFFIC SWERVING—COLLIDING—AS A MASSIVE DISPLAY OF VEHICLES—**MADLY HYDROPLANE**—THE SUV SPINS ACROSS LANES— SLOWING JUST ENOUGH TO REGAIN CONTROL—PENGUIN SNAPS HIS HEAD TO SEE—THE BATMOBILE CRESTING THE

EMBANKMENT—PENGUIN PUNCHES IT—VEERING OFF DOWN THE FLOODED HIGHWAY—WATER SPRAYING IN HIS WAKE—<u>BATMOBILE BARRELLING AFTER</u>—!!!

PENGUIN **SLALOMS RECKLESSLY** THROUGH SPEEDING TRAFFIC—BARELY MAINTAINING CONTROL—HIS CRAZED EYES FLIT TO THE REARVIEW—THE BATMOBILE RELENTLESSLY MATCHING HIM—MOVE FOR MOVE— DESPERATE, PENGUIN STREAKS AHEAD—SUDDENLY WALLED IN BY—

<u>A LONG LINE OF EIGHTEEN-WHEELERS</u> <u>CHUGGING AT HIGH SPEED</u>—PENGUIN GLANCES BACK—<u>THE BATMOBILE GAINING</u>—NOWHERE TO GO NOW—TRAPPED—WHEN— PENGUIN DOES SOMETHING <u>CRAZY</u>—ACCELARATING <u>EVEN FASTER</u>—PAST THE LEAD TRUCK—**JERKING RIGHT IN FRONT OF HIM**—THE TRUCK SCREECHES— **IMMEDIATELY HYDROPLANING**—<u>SETTING OFF</u> **A CHAIN REACTION**!

BATMAN SEES **THE HORRIFYING SIGHT OF MASSIVE TRUCKS AHEAD ALL JACKKNIFING**—ONE AFTER ANOTHER—<u>THE BATMOBILE HEADING STRAIGHT FOR UNAVOIDABLE, CATACLYSMIC COLLISION</u>!

BATMAN SEIZES THE NITROUS LINE TRIGGER— SQUEEZING IT—<u>THE BATMOBILE SUDDENLY LAUNCHING</u> **TOWARD THE TRUCKS**—BATMAN <u>YANKING THE WHEEL</u>—**SKIDDING INTO A CRAZY DRIFT**—

PENGUIN LOOKS BACK—<u>AS THE TRUCKS ALL CONVERGE AROUND THE DOOMED, CAREENING BATMOBILE, OBSCURING IT FROM VIEW</u>—

PENGUIN

HA! I GOT YOU! TAKE THAT
YOU FRIGGIN' PSYCHO—**I GOT
YOU**—!

WHEN—TO PENGUIN'S SHOCK—**THE BATMOBILE
REAPPEARS**—TWO WHEELS FLIPPING UP ONTO THE
CENTER DIVIDER—THE TILTED CAR SHOOTING THROUGH
THE NARROW SPACE ON THE SHOULDER BESIDE THE
EXPANDING PILE-UP—THE BATMOBILE BARELY
CLEARING THE DESTRUCTION—PENGUIN'S EYES WIDEN—
AS IT SWERVES OFF THE DIVIDER—**RIGHT AT THE
ESCALADE**—

PENGUIN

HOLY SHIIIIIIIIIIII—!!!

KA-BLAMMMM! THE BATMOBILE RAMS SAVAGELY INTO THE ESCALADE—THE TWO VEHICLES LOCKING TOGETHER **AS THEY SPINNNN**—!

ON BATMAN—WORLD BLURRING AROUND HIM—BATMOBILE SHAKING—<u>AS HE KEEPS HIS FOOT FURIOUSLY ON THE GAS</u>—

UNTIL FINALLY—THE TWO VEHICLES SMASH STRAIGHT INTO A LINE OF YELLOW OFF-RAMP CRASH BARRELS—THE BATMOBILE DISENGAGING—AS THE **ESCALADE FLIPS**—

INSIDE THE ESCALADE

THE PENGUIN—ROLLS OVER—AND OVER—AND OVER—TILL **SCRRRRAPE**... HE STOPS—UPSIDE-DOWN. PENGUIN bleeds—stunned—hearing only pounding rain now... He gazes out the window—disoriented to SEE... **UPSIDE-DOWN BAT BOOTS** <u>walking surreally into view on the road right outside</u>—BATMAN crouches slowly into frame—Penguin's bloodshot eyes widening—as Batman leans in eerily—<u>and thrusts a HOOD over his face</u>—SWALLOWING US IN BLACKNESS—

EXT. DESERTED GOTHAM TRAIN YARD—NIGHT

<u>PENGUIN'S HEAD SLAMS INTO THE SIDE OF A TRAIN CAR</u>—THE HOOD is yanked off—he looks around in panic—hands and feet bound—<u>BATMOBILE'S HEADLIGHTS IN HIS FACE</u>—Batman looms in near silhouette before him—as a FIGURE gets out of another car, joining ominously; <u>it's Gordon</u>.

> PENGUIN
> ...Jesus... the hell <u>is</u> this...? Good cop... <u>bat-shit cop</u>?!

BATMAN

Who's The Riddler?

PENGUIN

Riddler?? How should I know—
???

GORDON

—let's make it easy for you,
Oz—cops caught you doin'
somethin'—they were gonna
shut you down—put you away—
so you gave up a bigger fish to
save your ass—

BATMAN

—you ratted out Salvatore
Maroni—his drops operation—

GORDON

—but then the cops and city
officials—the mayor—the D.A.—
they all got greedy, right?

Wasn't enough to score a big
career-making bust—they could
take over the drops business
too—but they needed a minor
league mope like you to run it—

BATMAN

—you don't just work for
Carmine Falcone—you work for
THEM too—

PENGUIN

—WHAT ARE YOU, CRAZY —?!

GORDON

That why you killed the girl—?!

PENGUIN

—I didn't kill ANYBODY!

BATMAN

—we know she worked for you at the 44 Below—

GORDON

—she got too close, right? She found out from Mitchell you were the rat—so you killed her— but somehow Riddler knows too—he knows so much about you—you must know about him—

BATMAN

—who is he—?!

PENGUIN

—BOY, you guys're a HELLUVA duet here—why don'cha start HARMONIZIN'?!

Only one problem with your little scenario, OK? I AIN'T NO RAT! YOU GOT ANY IDEA WHAT CARMINE FALCONE WOULD DO TO ME IF HE **HEARD** THIS KINDA TALK?!

GORDON

Oh—you don't wanna talk about
rats? Why don't we talk about
what they DID to my partner's
face?!

GRUESOME CRIME SCENE PHOTOS are thrust in Penguin's
face:

PENGUIN

Holy GOD, whattaya SHOWIN'
me—?!

GORDON

PAY ATTENTION—this was
around his head, OK?! It's a
RAT'S maze—

PENGUIN

—OHHHH...!

GORDON

OPEN YOUR EYES—!!!

GORDON

ARE **YOU** EL RATA ALADA—?!

PENGUIN

—EL RATA ALADA—?!?!?

GORDON

Yeah, a RAT with wings—a stool
pigeon—that's not you?! These
symbols in the maze—right
here—says: "YOU ARE EL RATA
ALADA"!

"You are EL rata"?! It SAYS that?!

WHY—got something ya wanna
TELL us, Oz—?!

—YEAH!!! THAT'S LIKE THE
WORST SPANISH I EVER
HEARD—!!!

...what—??!

—it's LA! LA rata—what, is this
Riddler STUPID or somethin'?!

Thrown, Gordon loses steam as Batman silently takes the
maze photo—eyeing the cipher—Gordon watches him—

Jesus—look at you two—world's
greatest detectives—am I the
only one here knows the
difference between EL and LA?
¿NO HABLA ESPAÑOL,
FELLAS?!

DO ME A FAVOR, SHITHEAD!
SHUT UP!

Penguin falls silent; Gordon steps over to Batman—

GORDON
...think he made a mistake?

BATMAN
(studying cipher)
He doesn't make mistakes...

PENGUIN
A rat with wings?! You know
what that sounds like to ME? A
friggin' BAT—you ever think of
THAT?!

BATMAN
—"you are el rata"—you... are...
el... it's a URL...

EXT. GORDON'S CAR—MOMENTS LATER

BATMAN AND GORDON gaze at the laptop which sits on the
roof—Batman types "**www.rataalada.com**" into the browser—
the SCREEN GOES BLACK—a dead link—?

GORDON
...maybe it was a mistake—
maybe he's not as smart as we—

BATMAN
—wait—

—A BLINKING PLAIN TEXT CURSOR appears alone on screen:

"<?>"

They watch it PULSE EERILY... when IT STARTS TYPING TEXT.

GORDON
—holy shit—is that <u>him</u>—?

—their eyes follow the cursor: "**did you find him?**"

Batman reaches for the keys... types: "**el rata alada?**" The cursor hesitates, blinking—then TYPES BACK: "**yes**"

Batman writes: "**maybe. is a penguin a rat with wings?**" Another pause—then MORE TEXT comes through: "**interesting**"—then—"**you're missing the big picture**"

GORDON
...the hell does <u>that</u> mean—<u>is</u> he,
or <u>isn't</u> he—?

Batman holds up a quieting hand, as another TEXT BEGINS: "i need to show you more for you to understand"—then: "my next victim is the biggest piece of the puzzle yet"

Gordon and Batman exchange a look of dread—Batman types: "**victim?**"—then—"**dead?**" The cursor pauses creepily; writes back: "**he will be soon**"—then—"**here's a clue to where you can find him...**"—the cursor writes out <u>A RIDDLE</u>—Gordon reads along:

GORDON (OS)
"**i grew up from a seed, tough
as a weed... but in a mansion, in
a slum... i'll never know where
i come from. do you know what
i am?**"

(then, to Batman)
...any idea...?

                    BATMAN
              ...yeah... he's an orphan...

Batman types: **"an orphan?"**—the cursor writes: **"good bye"**
and the SCREEN GOES BLACK. Something HAUNTS Batman:

                    BATMAN
              ..."a mansion, in a slum"... He's
              talking about the old
              orphanage...

                    GORDON
              —one that burned down?

                    BATMAN
              It was part of the Wayne estate...
              they donated it after they built
              the tower...

                    GORDON
              —let's go—

They start off—when—a VOICE cries from off-screen—

                    PENGUIN (OS)
              Hey—you guys REALIZE I'm still
              here, right—?!

REVEAL PENGUIN—hands and feet still helplessly bound—

                    PENGUIN
              You gonna UNTIE me—how'm I
              s'posed to get OUTTA here?!!!

—and they get into their cars—starting off—

                    PENGUIN
            YOU GODDAMN
            SONSABITCHES—!!!

INT. BATMOBILE—MOVING—NIGHT

APPROACHING A FADED SIGN: "**A GOTHAM RENEWAL PROJECT—INVESTING IN OUR FUTURE**" BATMAN SLOWS, arriving at THE BURNT-DOWN REMAINS OF THE GOTHAM ORPHANAGE...

INT. MAIN ENTRYWAY—GOTHAM ORPHANAGE RUINS—NIGHT

BLACKNESS SHATTERS as the front doors are KICKED IN— Batman and Gordon stare in... Gordon raises his GUN—

                    BATMAN
            No guns...

                    GORDON
            Yeah, man... that's your thing...

And THEY ENTER... scanning black walls and floors—rain drips inside—Gordon's beam lands on WHITE-PAINTED ARROWS FRESHLY SCRAWLED over soot; he pans along them—to A GOTHIC STAIRCASE—Batman and Gordon exchange a look—begin FOLLOWING MORE ARROWS UP THE STEPS TO—

A LONG FOREBODING HALLWAY OF DOORS UPSTAIRS

MORE ARROWS point on. Gordon sweeps his light into empty rooms—when they notice EERIE ECHOING IN THE DISTANCE—

...<u>what's that</u>...?

As they move closer, it sounds strangely like... <u>MUSIC</u>—<u>a</u>
<u>distant BOY'S CHOIR singing SHUBERT'S "**AVE MARIA**"!</u>
<u>WEIRD GIGGLING COMES SUDDENLY FROM **VERY**</u>
<u>CLOSE BY</u>—<u>THEY LIFT THEIR EYES TO</u>—<u>**A SILHOUETTED**</u>
<u>FIGURE</u> <u>EMERGING FROM A DOOR</u>—<u>IT FREEZES,</u>
<u>STARTLED TO SEE BATMAN AND GORDON</u>—

GORDON
HEY! <u>HEY</u>!!!

<u>THE FIGURE BOLTS TO ANOTHER ROOM</u>—<u>SLAMMING THE</u>
<u>DOOR</u>—<u>BATMAN AND GORDON ALREADY CHASING</u>—
<u>GORDON RAISING HIS GUN</u>—<u>SMASHING THE DOOR</u>—<u>THEY</u>
<u>LOOK INSIDE TO SEE</u>...

...<u>A GROUP OF DROPS ADDICTS</u> SPRAWLED on melted metal
bed frames, FACES CONTORTED IN FROZEN GRINS; one
GIGGLES in a daze—Gordon swings his light to the Figure
from the hallway, who cowers, <u>gripping A BOTTLE AND</u>
<u>EYE-DROPPER</u>—

GORDON
Friggin' <u>dropheads</u>...

—when they hear—<u>CHEERS and APPLAUSE ring out as the</u>
<u>DISTANT SINGING STOPS</u>—**A MAN'S VOICE** <u>BEGINS</u>
<u>ECHOING</u>—

ECHOING VOICE
Thank you! Thank you,
everyone! Thank you for coming
today...

GORDON
—the hell is that—?

SOMETHING IN THE ECHOING VOICE STRIKES BATMAN—
Gordon watches surprised—AS BATMAN STARTS TOWARD
THE SOUND—

MOVE WITH HIM to the END OF THE HALL, near the sound
of the VOICE—Batman looks up, haunted; white paint above
the doorway says: "**WHERE IT ALL BEGAN**"—he STEPS
INTO—

A GRAND HALL—HIGH WIDE ANGLE

Batman dwarfed by the massive, burnt-out room; he squints
at A BEAM OF LIGHT, SPARKLING THROUGH DRIPPING
RAIN—it's from a cheap, MINI USB PROJECTOR on a tiny
tripod—Batman looks at the wall where AN OLD GC1 CLIP
FLICKERS—the MAN WITH THE ECHOING VOICE gives a
speech in front of a BOY'S CHOIR IN THE VERY ROOM
BATMAN NOW STANDS IN—a CHYRON explains why
Batman is so affected—**it's THOMAS WAYNE**. Batman
watches, unnerved—staring at a ghost—

THOMAS WAYNE
I believe in Gotham. I believe in
its promise. But too many have
been left behind for too long.
And that's why I'm here today to
announce, not only my
candidacy for mayor, but also
the creation of the Gotham
Renewal Fund. Win or lose, the
Wayne Foundation pledges a

one billion dollar donation to start a charitable endowment for public works. I want to bypass political gridlock to get money to people and projects who need it now—like these children behind me. Renewal is about growth. It's about planting seeds. And renewing Gotham's promise.

Batman is struck by the sight of TEN-YEAR-OLD BRUCE beside his MOTHER—Batman's eyes drift to more white painted words on the wall beside the projected image— "**RENEWAL IS A LIE**"—Batman stares, disturbed—WHEN A VOICE behind startles him out of his reverie—

> VOICE (OS)
> —sins of the father…?

BATMAN SPINS—it's GORDON—he follows Gordon's gaze to MORE WRITING on the wall: "**THE SINS OF THE FATHER…**"

> BATMAN
> …shall be visited upon the son.

Gordon walks closer, staring, as he gets it too…

> GORDON
> …Jesus… his next victim is…
> Bruce Wayne—

He turns for confirmation—**BUT BATMAN IS ALREADY GONE**.

SMASH TO:

A PHONE RINGING—SOMEWHERE IN WAYNE TOWER—
NIGHT

IT **RINGS** TWICE—but no one comes to answer—the tiny
illuminated SCREEN FLASHING—"NO CALLER ID"—

SMASH TO:

INSIDE THE SPEEDING BATMOBILE—NIGHT

ENGINE ROARING—WE HEAR **RINGING** ON HANDS-
FREE—Batman staring at his phone—willing someone to pick
up—

**BACK TO ALFRED ALONE IN THE STUDY—WAYNE TOWER—
NIGHT**

WE HEAR **ONLY THE INSISTENT RINGING** OF THE
PHONE—as Alfred opens piles of mail—when he
NOTICES—A BULGING MANILA MAILER—he picks it up,
curious... reads the SCRAWLED LETTERING: "PERSONAL/
CONFIDENTIAL—FOR BRUCE WAYNE'S EYES ONLY" ...
starts to OPEN IT...

SMASH TO:

REFLECTIONS RACING OVER THE BATMOBILE'S WINDSHIELD

BATMAN NOW SCREAMING—BUT ALL WE HEAR IS THE
RINGING PHONE—AS THE BATMOBILE RIPS INTO THE
ROLLING PARK—

ALFRED

pulls a GIFT-WRAPPED BOX from the mailer... sees A SILVER
ENVELOPE taped to it—HIS EYES WIDEN IN SHOCK as he
discovers the envelope reads... **"FOR THE BATMAN"**—

THE INSISTENT PHONE GROWING <u>LOUDER</u>—<u>LIKE A WARNING</u>—as he flips the envelope—PUZZLED TO FIND A LABEL: "<u>FIREPROOF</u>"—ALARMED—ALFRED GLANCES AT THE GIFT-WRAPPED BOX—<u>SEES **WIRES PROTRUDING FROM THE PAPER**</u>—

BACK TO THE PHONE

<u>THE **RINGING FINALLY STOPS**—AS A WOMAN'S HAND PICKS UP</u>—

> DORY (OS)
>
> ...hello—?

INT. BATMOBILE—IMMEDIATELY

> BATMAN
>
> <u>Dory—I need to speak to Alfred!</u>

> DORY (OVER PHONE)
>
> —oh—Mr. <u>Wayne</u>—

> BATMAN
>
> <u>**LISTEN** TO ME—SOMETHING **TERRIBLE'S** GOING TO HAPPEN</u>!

CLOSE ON DORY, HOLDING THE PHONE

> —for the first time we see her face; <u>she's distraught</u>—

                          DORY
              I'm afraid it... already <u>has</u>, sir.

BATMAN

LIFTS HIS EYES WITH DREAD AS—<u>WAYNE TOWER COMES
INTO VIEW</u>—<u>BLACK SMOKE PLUMES FROM AN UPPER
FLOOR</u>—<u>FIREMEN AIM HOSES FROM TELESCOPIC
LADDERS</u>—<u>DOUSING FLAMES</u>—

BACK TO ALFRED IN THE STUDY—FLEETING—A WIDE SHOT

STANDING WITH THE PACKAGE ONE LAST SECOND—
TOSSING IT—<u>HE DIVES</u>—AS THE PACKAGE **SILENTLY
ERUPTS**—WE HEAR—

                    DORY (OVER PHONE)
                 ...about an <u>hour</u> ago...

BACK TO BATMAN

<u>rocked, realizing he never had a chance to save him</u>—

THEN BACK TO DORY

as anguished tears begin to spill—

                          DORY
               ...I'm so sorry... I've been trying
                     to <u>reach</u> you...

As A BLUR WIPES in front of her TO REVEAL **EMERGENCY
PERSONNEL SWARMING** the stairs of a LOWER TOWER
LANDING—

HUSHED GCPD DETECTIVE
(PRELAP)
The package was intended for
you.

INT. WAYNE TOWER—GRAND FOYER—NIGHT

Bruce, stunned as DETECTIVES speak in the AFTERMATH:

HUSHED GCPD DETECTIVE
...we found this too...

He shows Bruce the SILVER ENVELOPE: **"TO THE BATMAN"**;
then pulls out A HEAT-SCORCHED GREETING CARD WITH
CARTOON EYES—Bruce looks—SCRAWLED inside is **"SEE**
YOU IN HELL"

HUSHED GCPD DETECTIVE
Any reason you'd be a target...?

ON BRUCE as he just stares at the words, stunned...

INT. HOSPITAL—WINDOW OUTSIDE AN I.C.U. ROOM—NIGHT

Bruce gazes through the glass at Alfred, bandaged and unconscious, breathing through an oxygen mask as NURSES attend to him; a DOCTOR emerges, moves to Bruce, grave...

> DOCTOR
> We've sedated him, we just have
> to hope he stabilizes. You should
> go home, Mr. Wayne, get some
> sleep.

Bruce nods, but it's not clear he's even heard what the doctor said; the doctor stares at him... says gently...

> DOCTOR
> Is there... anyone else to notify...
> next of kin?

Finally, Bruce turns, disoriented...

> BRUCE
> ...no, it's... just me...

INT. WAYNE TOWER—DINING ROOM—EARLY MORNING

A HEAVY TABLE SCRAPES across the tiled floor—WE HEAR a **HISS OF A SPRAY CAN**—AS **WHITE LINES** SPRAY ON THE TILE—

CLOSE ON **PHOTOS—MAYOR AND ANNIKA—COMMISSIONER AND THE DROPS PUSHER**—SCRAWLED **WORDS—MITCHELL—SAVAGE—COLSON**—WHEN THE **HISSING STOPS**—AS WE REVEAL—**BRUCE**, shirtless, on hands and knees, spray can in hand, staring down at something on the floor, **UTTERLY TORTURED**—as he begins to rise slowly to his feet—we see—THE DINING ROOM FLOOR IS NOW A **MASSIVE EVIDENCE BOARD**—lines connect details—HE'S FROZEN on one area—it says: **"THE SINS OF MY FATHER"**, followed by **"???"**

ON BRUCE'S EYES as they bore into the words... then, shift intensely to another phrase—**"RENEWAL IS A LIE"**

INT. WAYNE TOWER—THE STUDY—MOMENTS LATER

YELLOW CRIME SCENE TAPE BREAKS AS BRUCE ENTERS—MOVING past the charred aftermath of the explosion—to A HUGE ANTIQUE WOOD CABINET—he opens a LONG DRAWER—

CLOSE ON LEGAL FILES—as FINGERS DIG to FIND a TAB: **"RENEWAL"**—BRUCE RIFLES THROUGH—OPENS THE NEXT DRAWER—MORE "RENEWAL" FILES—THE NEXT—MORE...

ON BRUCE AT THE STUDY DESK—SHORT TIME LATER

WALLED IN by ENORMOUS STACKS OF FILES—Bruce searching them—he closes one—fumbling for another—when a huge stack BEGINS TO TOPPLE—he LURCHES to save it—KNOCKING OVER MORE—thousands of pages spilling—Bruce watches, helpless as they scatter everywhere—

He stands there, watching it all settle... FINALLY, HE SNAPS—HURLING OVER the other stacks—PAPER EXPLODING EVERYWHERE—BRUCE'S PENT-UP FURY UNLEASHED—SMASHING UP THE ROOM, DESTROYING EVERYTHING—FURNITURE—ART—HIS RAGE IS TERRIFYING—even as he begins to EXHAUST HIMSELF—running out of things to smash—but not sated, searching for more—when he sees SOMETHING...

ALFRED'S MONOGRAMMED **W** CUFFLINK. If Bruce would ever allow himself to cry, it would be now... he stares, stone-faced at the link, eyes just beginning to well...

INT. BATCAVE—AFTERNOON

Bruce sets down Renewal files on his work bench, lifting his laptop screen—when he notices AN OPEN WINDOW—the contact lens interface—but now there is A LIVE IMAGE—a HANDWRITTEN SIGN faces camera: "**WHERE R U?**" Surprised, Bruce picks up the ear piece—

> BRUCE
> ...Selina...?

SELINA appears—staring blindly at the camera—

> SELINA
> Can you see me...?

> BRUCE
> ...Yeah.

> SELINA
> (harried, urgent)
> I need to talk. Where can we go?

EXT. UNFINISHED SKYSCRAPER—HIGH OVER THE CITY—SUNSET

Batman's silhouette, gazing darkly at Gotham—when the elevator arrives—he turns as Selina emerges in her cat suit, removing her wind mask. He looks at her with edge—

BATMAN

Cat burglar pulling another
score?

SELINA

It's not safe for me here now.

BATMAN

Wasn't sure I'd see you again.

SELINA

Yeah well, things were getting a
little hot for me...

(then)
How could they <u>do</u> that to her—?
I'm gonna <u>find</u> them, make them
<u>pay</u>—that piece of shit, Kenzie,
all of 'em. <u>You gonna help me?</u>

BATMAN

...help you?

SELINA

Yeah! I thought you were
"<u>Vengeance</u>"—

BATMAN

Your friend got involved with
the wrong people—she didn't
know better. Maybe you should
have explained it to her...

SELINA

The hell's <u>that</u> supposed to
mean?

                    BATMAN
It means your choices have
consequences—

                    SELINA
—oh, Jesus Christ—<u>choices</u>?!

You know, whoever the hell you
are, obviously, <u>you grew up rich</u>.

He just stares back—giving nothing away—

                    BATMAN
...was it worth it?

                    SELINA
What?

                    BATMAN
Compromising yourself for
money.

<u>She glares at him</u>—

                    BATMAN
What'd you have to <u>do</u> to set up
that score? How close did you
have to <u>get</u>? To Penguin—to
<u>Falcone</u>?

                    SELINA
—you don't know what the <u>hell</u>
you're talking about, OK?!—
<u>Falcone owes me that money</u>—!

                    BATMAN
—<u>owes</u> you—?

                    SELINA
            —yeah—and a lot more!

                    BATMAN
            —oh really—why's that?

                    SELINA
               (moving to leave)
            —forget it—I can't even talk to
            you—!

                    BATMAN
               (grabs her hard)
            —no—tell me—I wanna know—
            why would a guy like Falcone
            owe you ANYthing—?!

                    SELINA
            —BECAUSE HE'S MY FATHER!

Batman falls silent, stunned—she shrugs him off... stands
there, eyes burning... then, quietly:

                    SELINA
            ...my... mother worked at the 44
            Below... just like Anni. She used
            to take me there when I was a
            little girl...

                    BATMAN
            ...to the club?

                    SELINA
            ...I hid out in the dressing room
            while she worked. I used to see
            him there... He scared the shit

out of me. I could never
understand why he looked at
me the way he did. Then one
night, my mother told me... who
he was.

He studies her as she gazes out at the skyline...

> SELINA
> When I was seven, my mother
> was murdered... Someone
> strangled her, they never found
> out who, probably some creep
> from the club. Anyway, when
> Social Services came to take me
> away, he didn't say a thing.
> Couldn't even look at me.
>
> (looks up at him)
> <u>He owes me that money</u>.

He looks at her, taking her in for the first time; nods:

> BATMAN
> ...sorry. For what I said...

She smiles. Studies his eyes.

> SELINA
> 's alright... you just assume the
> worst in people... Maybe we
> aren't so different after all...
>
> (running a finger along his mask)
> Who are you under there?

What're you hiding? Are you
just... hideously scarred?

BATMAN
(beat, eyes on hers)
...yeah.

He smiles. She smiles back. Chemistry between them. Then:

SELINA
Listen to me... if we don't stand
up for Anni, no one will. All
anyone cares about in this place
are these... white... privileged
assholes—the mayor, the
commissioner, the D.A.—and
now Thomas and Bruce Wayne.
Far as I'm concerned, that
psycho's right to go after these
creeps—I'd think you'd be on
his side—!

BATMAN
—wait, what do you—what do
you mean Thomas and Bruce
Wayne?

SELINA
What, do you live in a cave? The
Riddler's latest—it's all about
the Waynes...

He's silently struck—but Selina doesn't even notice—

SELINA

Listen—if I can find that dickbag
Kenzie, will you help me?

He looks at her, reeling—sees her pleading eyes—

SELINA
(quiet, intimate)
Please... Come on, "Vengeance"...

BATMAN
(finally nods; then)
But don't make any moves
without me—understand—this
is all more dangerous than you
know—

—she cuts him off with a LONG KISS... then pulls slowly
back... staring into his eyes, whispering with a smile—

SELINA

I told you, baby, I can take care
of myself...

And she starts off—he watches her go... as we hear—

A MAN'S VOICE (VO)

I'm Thomas Wayne, and I
approve this message...

As Copland's "FANFARE FOR THE COMMON MAN" begins—

INT. "THE CAVE"—UNDERNEATH WAYNE TOWER—NIGHT

BATMAN PULLS OFF HIS COWL—revealing Bruce, BLACK
CAMO AND SWEAT running down his face from around his
eyes; he stares, rattled, at GC1 on the huge LED TV—the
CHYRON reads: "**EXPLOSIVE NEW RIDDLER VIDEO GOES
VIRAL**"—below that: "**Killer's message has over 13 million
views**"

THE VIDEO is A TWENTY-YEAR-OLD CAMPAIGN AD:
THOMAS WAYNE at the orphanage, MARTHA and YOUNG
BRUCE beside him—

THOMAS WAYNE

From a very young age, my
family—Martha's family, the
Arkhams—instilled in both of
us... that giving back is not just
an obligation... it's a passion.
That is our families' legacy—

The IMAGE FREEZES—EERIE MUSIC swallowing the
"Fanfare" as the video takes on the tone of a political attack
ad—VINTAGE FAMILY PHOTOS of the WAYNES and
ARKHAMS appear—

> RIDDLER (VO)
> (eerie VOICE CHANGER)
> The Waynes and the Arkhams—
> Gotham's founding families...
> but what is their <u>real</u> legacy...?

—the photos bleed RED—turning DARKER—as a GOTHAM GAZETTE REPORTER'S BYLINE PHOTO fades up—

> RIDDLER (VO)
> Twenty years ago, one reporter
> set out to uncover the <u>dark
> truth</u>...
>
> He found <u>shocking family
> secrets</u>.

FLASHES OF POLICE and **AUTOPSY PHOTOS** FILL THE SCREEN—

> RIDDLER (VO)
> How when Martha was just a
> child, her mother brutally
> <u>murdered her father</u>, then
> committed <u>suicide</u>—and how the
> Arkhams used their power and
> money <u>to cover it up</u>...

WE SEE A DEATH CERTIFICATE; "**Cause of Death: ACCIDENTAL**"

> RIDDLER (VO)
> How Martha <u>herself</u> was in and
> out of institutions for years—
> <u>and they didn't want anyone to
> know</u>...

SHOTS OF AN INSTITUTION—spying through a fence at a
DISTURBED YOUNG WOMAN, SURROUNDED BY NURSES—

> RIDDLER (VO)
> Thomas Wayne tried to force
> this crusading reporter into a
> hush money agreement to save
> his mayoral campaign...

AS THOMAS SHAKES HANDS on the campaign trail—a
LEGAL DOCUMENT spins on screen—THE WORD "**HUSH!**"
APPEARS—

> RIDDLER (VO)
> But when the reporter refused,
> Wayne turned to longtime
> secret associate, mafia kingpin
> Carmine Falcone—and had him
> murdered...

A GUNSHOT RINGS OUT—NEWS FOOTAGE of the DEAD
REPORTER plays; the HEADLINE: "**GANG-LAND STYLE
EXECUTION**"—as a SUPER-ENLARGED PHOTO from the
orphanage dedication FADES UP: **THOMAS and CARMINE
FALCONE TALKING CONSPIRATORIALLY**—

> RIDDLER (VO)
> The Waynes and Arkhams—
> Gotham's legacy of lies—and
> murder...

We see A CAMPAIGN POSTER; "MAYOR" has been crossed
out, it reads: "THOMAS WAYNE FOR **MURDERER**".
RIDDLER appears—

                              RIDDLER
                    One by one, Gotham's Pillars
                    fall... on Judgement Day, the
                    wreckage will consume us all...

                    GOOD byyyyyyyye—

ON BRUCE, absolutely ROCKED—as CLUB MUSIC RISES—

BLACKNESS

SWINGS OPEN—REVEALING BRUCE—OUTSIDE THE CLUB—

                               BRUCE
                          Know who I am?

REVEAL ONE OF THE TWIN BOUNCERS—staring in shock—

                             BOUNCER
                       ...you're Bruce Wayne.

                               BRUCE
                    I wanna see Carmine Falcone.

The Bouncer just looks at him—then SHUTS THE DOOR—
BEAT—the DOOR OPENS: BOTH TWINS standing there
now—

                             BOUNCER
                        (looking at his Twin)
                    See...?

The Twin stares in disbelief as Bruce glares; then breaks into
an excited smile, like he's seeing a rock star—

                          TWIN BOUNCER
                         ...c'mon in.

**INT. FALCONE'S SHORELINE LOFT—PRIVATE ELEVATOR—
NIGHT**

The doors open; we FOLLOW BRUCE down a long hallway to
A DRAWING ROOM; HOODS and HOSPITALITY WOMEN
crowd around a pool table, drinking, playing—at the table,
CARMINE FALCONE looks over to see Bruce, the Twins
behind him—Bruce glowers silently at Falcone, who stares
back with a smirk... when the others begin to notice,
quieting...

> FALCONE
> Give us a minute, fellas.

The BODYGUARDS usher everyone out.

> FALCONE
> Have a seat...

But Bruce just stands there.

> FALCONE
> Thought I might hear from you.
> This Riddler sonuvabitch is
> really stirring things up, isn't
> he—?

> BRUCE
> (quiet)
> Is it true?

> FALCONE
> What? ...that reporter business?

A beat. Falcone studies Bruce's rage-filled eyes.

FALCONE
Whattaya wanna know here,
kid? Whattaya lookin' for?

BRUCE
The truth. Did you kill him. For
my father.

FALCONE
Look, your father saved my life. I
was loyal to him. I even trieda
give money to his campaign, and
that whole Renewal thing—but
he wouldn't take it. He didn't
wanna associate with a guy like
me—

BRUCE
My father hated everything you
stand for.

FALCONE
(smiles)
Yeah, I know. Course he did.
Guys like you, your father, you
don't want anything to do with
me...

(darkens, bitter)
...til you need me. Right?

A beat as they look at each other.

FALCONE
Your father was in trouble, OK?
This reporter had some dirt,

some very personal stuff about your mother, her family history... you know, everybody's got their dirty laundry, that's how it is. But he didn't want none of that coming out, not right before the election. Your father trieda pay this guy off, but he wasn't goin' for it. So he came to me. I never seen him like that. He said: <u>I want you to put the fear of God in this guy</u>.

Bruce stares, unnerved...

> FALCONE
>
> And when fear isn't enough, you take it to the next level. Your father wanted me to handle it.
>
> (a shark's eyes)
> So I did. I handled it.

Bruce is truly unmoored; Falcone enjoying his pain...

> FALCONE
>
> I know, you thought your father was a boy scout. But you'd be surprised what even a "good" man like him is capable of. In the right situation.
>
> (then)
> Do me a favor, don't lose any sleep over this, OK? This reporter was a <u>lowlife</u>, he was

on <u>Maroni's payroll</u>—he got
what was comin'.

                    BRUCE
...<u>Maroni</u>?

                    FALCONE
Oh yeah. Maroni could never
stand your father and I had
history. And after what
happened with this reporter,
I think he was worried your
father would be in my pocket
forever. He woulda done
<u>anything</u> to keep him from
becoming mayor.

          (a pointed beat)
Ya understand?

Bruce shakes his head, reeling,
resisting the notion...

                    FALCONE
...<u>sure</u> ya do...

                    BRUCE
Are you saying...? Salvatore
Maroni... <u>had my father killed</u>?

Falcone lets that just hang in the air... then:

                    FALCONE
Do I know it for a <u>fact</u>...? I'm just
sayin', <u>it sure looked that way
to me</u>.

As the shock hits Bruce... Falcone regards him coldly...

>   FALCONE
> This what you wanted? This
> little conversation here?

Bruce can't even respond...

>   FALCONE (OS)
> Anhh... I spose it's been a long
> time comin'... I mean you ain't a
> kid no more...

INT. WAYNE TOWER—GRAND FOYER—DAWNING LIGHT

Bruce arrives at the top of the stairs in a daze, stops, staring at... the CHAINED and PADLOCKED SET OF DOORS...

INT. BRUCE'S PARENTS' DARKENED BEDROOM—MOMENTS LATER

Untouched in twenty years... a frozen moment, covered in dust. Bruce enters, taking in the unbearable stillness... In the early light, he sees a man's suit jacket draped on a chair... a pair of glasses rest on an old newspaper... He turns, seeing a STAINED TEACUP, askew in its saucer on a woman's dressing table... behind it, on the mirror, are yellowed CHILDREN'S CRAYON DRAWINGS: his... One's a stick-figure, smiling family... a mother, father, and child...

A quiet HEART MONITOR BEEPING begins as Bruce stares...

INT. ALFRED'S HOSPITAL ROOM—TWILIGHT

Alfred opens his eyes to see BRUCE seated at his bedside, rumpled. Bruces smiles sadly, finally speaking, pained:

                    BRUCE
        ...you lied to me. My whole life.

            (long, pregnant beat)
        I... spoke to Carmine Falcone...

Pain and shock fill Alfred's eyes... he blinks away; then back.
Finally, he struggles for voice... hoarse...

                    ALFRED
        ...what'd he... <u>say</u>...?

                    BRUCE
        ...he... told me what he did... for
        my father... and about Salvatore
        Maroni.

Alfred's eyes burn... trying to understand...

                    ALFRED
        ...he told you... Salvatore
        Maroni...?

                    BRUCE
        ...had my father killed.

Alfred just gazes, pained.

                    BRUCE
        Alfred, why didn't you <u>tell</u> me
        all this...? I spent all these years
        <u>fighting</u> for him... believing he
        was a <u>good man</u>—

                    ALFRED
        —he <u>was</u> a good man—

Bruce shakes his head—but Alfred grows more fierce—

> **ALFRED**
> —listen to me... your <u>father</u>...
> was a <u>good man</u>—he... made a
> <u>mistake</u>—

> **BRUCE**
> A mistake? He had a man
> killed—<u>why</u>—to protect the
> <u>family image</u>—his <u>political</u>
> <u>aspirations</u>—?

> **ALFRED**
> —it <u>wasn't</u> to protect the family
> image—and he <u>DIDN'T have</u>
> <u>anyone killed</u>...

The forcefulness of that makes Bruce stop—he looks at
Alfred... who continues, simply, emotional...

> **ALFRED**
> <u>He was protecting your mother</u>.
> He didn't care about his image,
> the campaign, any of that. He
> cared about <u>her</u>. <u>And you</u>.
> These... ...secrets about your
> mother's family, they haunted
> her, she'd battled them every
> single day. We all have our
> scars, Bruce. And your father
> knew, if everything came out,
> it'd be too much for her. It would
> <u>destroy</u> her. He just... he loved

her so much. And in a moment
of weakness, he turned to
Falcone. <u>But he never thought
Falcone would kill that man.</u>
Your father should have known
that Falcone would do anything
to finally <u>have</u> something on him
he could <u>use</u>... <u>to own him.</u> That's
who Falcone is. And that was
your father's mistake.

(then)
But when Falcone told him what
he'd done, your father was
distraught—he told Falcone he
was going to the police, that'd
he'd confess <u>everything</u>... And
that night... your father and
your mother were killed.

Bruce is stunned...

                    BRUCE
...it was... <u>Falcone</u>...?

Alfred looks at him sadly, so wanting to give Bruce the
answer he <u>needs, the answer he's wanted his whole life</u>...

                    ALFRED
...I wish I... knew for <u>sure</u>... Yes...
<u>maybe</u>... Or maybe it was some
random <u>thug</u> on the street who
needed money, who got <u>scared</u>
and pulled the trigger too fast...
<u>If you don't think I've spent</u>

<u>every day searching for that</u>
<u>answer</u>...

(truly distraught)
It was <u>my job</u> to protect them—
do you understand? I know you
always blamed yourself. You
were only a boy, Bruce. I could
see the <u>fear</u> in your eyes. But I
didn't know how to <u>help</u>. I could
teach you to <u>fight</u>—but I wasn't
prepared to <u>take care</u> of you.
You needed a father. But all you
had... was me. I'm sorry...

Alfred averts his eyes, red with heartbreak and regret. Bruce
stares at him, deeply affected...

BRUCE
...no, Alfred... don't be sorry...

(then, quiet, struck)
God, I... never thought I'd feel
fear like that again... I thought
I'd mastered all that. I mean, I'm
not afraid to die...

His unflinching gaze meets Alfred's, who nods, solemn... then,
Bruce's eyes shift away again, processing...

BRUCE
But I realize now, there's
something I never got past... The
fear of... ever going through <u>any</u>
of that again...

> (looking at Alfred)
> ...<u>of losing someone I care about</u>.

Alfred looks back, moved—he smiles, tears in his eyes:

> **ALFRED**
> Well... I'm afraid you won't be
> rid of me just yet...

Bruce smiles sadly back... then gazes off...

> **BRUCE**
> I went into their room last night.

Alfred is quietly struck.

> **BRUCE**
> It all... seemed so much smaller.

Alfred watches Bruce, a fleeting glimpse of the man as a boy...
He reaches out a hand. Bruce stares, surprised... then lifts
his own... clasping Alfred's tightly... Then Bruce darkens...
noticing something outside the window... Alfred turns... <u>sees
the BAT-SIGNAL IN THE SKY</u>.

EXT. ABANDONED SKYSCRAPER CONSTRUCTION SITE—NIGHT

The Batmobile arrives—emerging to see—<u>Gordon, getting out
of his car too—they trade confused looks</u>—

> **GORDON**
> ...<u>hey</u>...

> **BATMAN**
> ...I... saw the signal—that's not
> <u>you</u>...?

> GORDON
>
> I thought it was you...

They both lift their eyes to the spotlight in the sky—

INT. RISING CONSTRUCTION ELEVATOR—SECONDS LATER

We hear SCREAMS as THE UPPER FLOOR COMES INTO VIEW—and GLIMPSE SELINA IN CAT SUIT, VICIOUSLY KICKING SOMEONE—Shocked, Batman and Gordon rush from the lift—

ONTO THE UNFINSHED FLOOR

Where Selina has a PRISONER BOUND BY HER LOCK CHAIN to the GUARDRAIL AT THE BUILDING'S EDGE— **KENZIE**—HIS FACE SWOLLEN—she's got his GLOCK in both hands—prowling, crazed—she sees Batman, spins—FIERCE—

> SELINA
>
> I found him—!

> BATMAN
>
> I see that—

> SELINA
>
> —what're we gonna do—he had
> my shit—my phone! She left a
> message! The night they took
> her—she called me—!

> KENZIE
> (totally freaked)
> Gordon! Help me OUT, man!

SELINA
(KICKS him again)
SHUT UP!!!

BATMAN
Put down the gun—

SELINA
—I'm telling you, goddammit—
she CALLED ME!

(pulling out PHONE)
Here—LISTEN!!!

She hits PLAY ON A VOICEMAIL—TOSSES THE PHONE to
Batman—Gordon steps closer—as **THE DISTORTED
MESSAGE PLAYS**: PANICKED BREATHING as an ANGRY
VOICE approaches—

MAN (OVER PHONE)
—back here—where you goin'!?

ANNIKA (OVER PHONE)
(terrified)
—n-n-nowhere—I—

—ANOTHER MAN'S VOICE joins—YELLING over them—

MAN TWO (OVER PHONE)
Hey-hey-HEY, whattaya doin'?
C'mon, Kenzie, you're scarin'
her.

MAN/KENZIE (OVER PHONE)
—oh, I'm—I'm sorry, Mr.
Falcone...

FALCONE (OVER PHONE)
(gentler)
Hey... you OK...? C'mere—

ANNIKA (OVER PHONE)
—please don't—don't hurt me—

FALCONE (OVER PHONE)
—don't be scared—c'mere...
Now, lemme just ask you again...
What'd Mitchell tell you...?

ANNIKA (OVER PHONE)
—n-nothing—he—

FALCONE (OVER PHONE)
Don liked to talk, I know that—
'specially to pretty girls like
you... that's why I made him take
your passport—till we could
have a little conversation—

ANNIKA (OVER PHONE)
—all I wanna do is get out of
here, OK? You'll never hear
from me again—nobody will—
PLEASE!

FALCONE (OVER PHONE)
We're gonna get you outta here,
I promise... But first, I gotta
know... what'd he tell you?

ANNIKA (OVER PHONE)
...he... he just said they... they all
made a... a deal with you—

> FALCONE (OVER PHONE)
> —ohhhh—he <u>told</u> you bout that,
> huh?—a <u>deal</u>—?

> ANNIKA (OVER PHONE)
> —yeah, long time ago he said—
> said you gave some information
> on some <u>drops thing</u> helped a lot
> of people—and that's how he
> became <u>mayor</u>—he said you
> were a... <u>very</u> important man...

> FALCONE (OVER PHONE)
> Right... uh-huh...

> (resigned sigh, then)
> OK...

AND SUDDENLY—**<u>ANNIKA BEGINS SHRIEKING</u>**—**<u>IT'S AGONIZING</u>**—BATMAN'S GAZE SHIFTS TO SELINA, WHO STARES OFF, TEARS BEGINNING—**<u>AS ANNIKA'S CRIES TURN TO DESPERATE GASPS</u>**—

> FALCONE (OVER PHONE)
> (strains, eerie calm)
> ...just... take it... easy—OK? Take
> it <u>easy</u>...

> GORDON
> Jesus... he's <u>strangling</u> her...

<u>SELINA'S EYES LIFT TO BATMAN'S</u>, ALIVE WITH RAGE— AS THE RECORDING FINALLY ENDS—EVERYONE SILENT. GORDON TURNS TO BATMAN, REELING—WHEN BATMAN'S EYES LIFT TO HIS:

BATMAN
…"rata alada". A falcon has
wings too. Falcone's the rat.

Gordon turns slowly to Kenzie; they move toward him—

GORDON
…he works for you guys? The
D.A.…? The mayor…?

Kenzie looks up at them, terrified… when… he cracks:

KENZIE
No… we work for him…
Everybody does…

BATMAN
HOW?

KENZIE
…through Renewal… Renewal is
everything—

GORDON
—the Renewal Fund…?

KENZIE
(shaking, it spills)
Yeah… After Thomas Wayne
died, they all went after it like
vultures—the mayor—Falcone—
Maroni—everyone got in on
it—it was perfect—for makin'
bribes—laundering money—a
huge charitable fund with no
oversight—everybody got a

piece. But Falcone wanted more.
So he orchestrated a play to take
Maroni down big—he'd rat out
his drops operation, make the
careers of everybody that went
after him, then install them all
as his puppets... He'd run the
city. And he's been doin' it ever
since—you think this goddamn
election matters? Falcone's the
mayor—he's been the mayor for
the last twenty years...

Selina turns to Batman: a truly scary look in her eyes—

SELINA
C'mon, "Vengeance"—let's go
kill that sonuvabitch—

(gun on Kenzie)
This creep too, let's finish this!

KENZIE
—OH, GOD—!!!

GORDON
—whoa—whoa—whoa!!!

—when a BLACK GLOVE knocks the gun to the floor!

BATMAN (OS)
No...

Selina spins, ready to strike, FACE TO FACE WITH
BATMAN—

                    BATMAN
          We'll get him, but not this way—

                    SELINA
          There is no other way—he owns
          the city!

                    BATMAN
          Cross that line... you'll become
          just like him...

Beside herself, she realizes—he's not with her—

                    BATMAN
          Listen to me—don't throw your
          life away—

Finally, she turns back to him—smiles, fatalistic—

                    SELINA
          Don't worry, honey—

With dancer's grace—she lifts a leg—touching her heel
provocatively to Kenzie's chest—then, hardening—

                    SELINA
          I got nine of 'em—

KENZIE'S EYES WIDEN—AS SHE KICKS HIM THROUGH
THE GUARDRAIL—KNOCKING HIM OFF THE BUILDING—!

GORDON LURCHES FORWARD ON INSTINCT—AS BATMAN
TRIGGERS HIS QUICK-DRAW SLIDER—FIRING A HARPOON
INTO KENZIE'S ANKLE—FIERCELY YANKING THE LINE
TAUT TO SAVE HIM—

KENZIE
JESUS CHRIIIIST—!!!

—AS BATMAN—STRUGGLING TO HOLD ON—SPINS TO
SEE—

SELINA LEAPING OFF THE EDGE WITH THE GLOCK—
LAUNCHING FOR A CABLE ON A CONSTRUCTION
CRANE—**JUST MAKING IT**—SLIDING DOWN THE LINE—
SWINGING OFF—**DISAPPEARING**!

—Gordon helps Batman pull a whimpering Kenzie back up—

Gordon turns to Batman—who's yanking a wired hook from
his belt—securing it on the edge—no time to lose—

GORDON
She'll never get outta there
alive—and if she kills Falcone,
we may never find The Riddler—

BATMAN
—I have to stop her—

GORDON
Don't you mean we—?

BATMAN
I gotta do this my way—

GORDON
And then what—?

Batman looks up as he finishes—

BATMAN
We do what Riddler said—

(tosses him SELINA'S PHONE)
<u>Bring the rat into the light</u>...

Gordon stares at the phone—<u>then nods, suddenly getting it</u>—as BATMAN JUMPS BACK—<u>RAPPELLING OFF THE TOWER</u>—

EXT. GOTHAM STREETS—AT HIGH SPEED—NIGHT

HURTLING down a service road under an elevated highway—REVEAL SELINA SCREECHING through the maze of columns on her bike—PAN as she SCREECHES PAST—heading toward—**THE ICEBERG LOUNGE**—<u>disappearing behind the building</u>—

EXT. DESERTED ALLEY BEHIND ICEBERG LOUNGE—SECONDS LATER

Selina whips off her helmet—ejects the Glock's clip to inspect rounds; SLAMS it back—UNZIPPING HER BODYSUIT—

THE BATMOBILE

ROARS on the service road—threading columns—when it
SKIDS TO A STOP—hidden in shadow—BATMAN peers at—

SELINA OUTSIDE THE CLUB, UNDER THE FLICKERING
STREET LAMP—now in HER SLIT DRESS—as <u>THE TWINS let
her in</u>—

SLOW ZOOM, BATMAN staring, intense, **deciding what
to do**—

INT. ICEBERG LOUNGE NIGHTCLUB—MOVING—NIGHT

MUSIC POUNDS AS WE MOVE TOWARD A GUARD beside
A PRIVATE ELEVATOR—his eyes brazenly check us out,
head to toe—

> SELINA
> (uncomfortable smile)
> <u>Hey</u>—could you tell Mr. Falcone
> I'd like to come up—

> ELEVATOR GUARD
> —he ain't seeing nobody tonight!

> SELINA
> (leans in, hushed)
> Just tell him it's about <u>Annika</u>...

He darkens—nods—Selina steps aside as he speaks low into a
mic on his sleeve. He opens the ELEVATOR DOOR for her—
watches... <u>AS SHE GETS IN</u>... <u>AND THE DOORS CLOSE</u>—

**INT. FALCONE'S SHORELINE LOFT—ELEVATOR HALLWAY—
NIGHT**

SELINA STEPS OUT, moving by an INTIMIDATING PHALANX OF GUARDS—to the DRAWING ROOM—where FALCONE APPEARS—

> FALCONE
>
> Look who it is—!

> SELINA
>
> —sorry to <u>bother</u> you—

> FALCONE
>
> No, it's <u>fine</u>, beautiful!

> SELINA
>
> I was just wondering if I could...
> <u>talk</u> to you for a minute... <u>alone</u>?

—and as we hear a LOUD POUNDING **KNOCK-KNOCK-KNOCK**—

BLACKNESS

SWINGS OPEN; we SEE OUTSIDE THE CLUB, <u>**BUT NO ONE'S THERE**</u>.

REVEAL THE TWINS staring out the door—confused—FOLLOW THEM OUT as they search for whoever was knocking—WHEN **BAM!**—they SPIN to SEE <u>THE DOOR SHUTTING THEM OUT</u>!

INT. HEART OF THE CLUB—MOVING—IMMEDIATELY

PUSHING THROUGH REVELERS—A FIGURE ENTERS FRAME—STRIDING in ARMY JACKET, CAP, and DUFFEL—<u>BATMAN HAS ENTERED AS **THE DRIFTER**—EYES SEARCHING—HE SPIES what he's been looking for—A DOOR: **"KEEP OUT"**</u>—ENTERS—

A SECURITY GUARD NOTICES—GIVING CHASE—MOVE WITH HIM—to see THE DRIFTER DISAPPEARING ROUND A CORNER—the GUARD DISAPPEARS AFTER HIM—HOLD in the empty corridor—when the GUARD'S BODY CRASHES OUT—**UNCONSCIOUS**—!

INT. FALCONE'S DRAWING ROOM—SAME TIME

Selina sits across from Falcone, who leans against the pool table, sizing her up as she grows emotional—

> SELINA
> ...I'm just—I'm so worried—I don't know where she is...! And I know you're a very important man, I was hoping maybe you could help me find her—I mean she's been gone so long, I'm starting to think she might be...
>
> (stops, tearing)
> —I'm so sorry—

> FALCONE
> (eyes her carefully)
> That's OK—I understand—

He offers her some tissues—

> SELINA
> No—thank you, I have some...

—as she reaches INTO HER CLUTCH ON HER LAP—where **THE GLOCK HIDES**—HER FINGERS STARTING TO **GRASP IT**—WHEN—

>   AN ALARMED VOICE (OS)
>   Mr. <u>Falcone</u>—!

—they both turn, startled, as a BALD BODYGUARD enters—
Selina eases off the gun, <u>taking out a Kleenex instead</u>—

>   FALCONE
>   Vinnie! Didn't I tell you I was—?

>   BALD BODYGUARD
>   I'm sorry, Mr. Falcone—I really
>   think you gonna wanna see
>   this...!

Falcone sees he's serious—nods—turns to Selina—

>   FALCONE
>   I'm sorry, beautiful—I'll be right
>   back...

Selina nods, wiping tears as he goes; she hardens as she looks
at the Glock, then leans to see...

<u>The Guard leading Falcone to a ROOM WHERE A TV PLAYS</u>—

BLACKNESS

A DOOR CRASHES OPEN REVEALING **THE CLUB
ELECTRICAL ROOM**—THE DUFFEL HITS THE FLOOR—THE
DRIFTER'S HANDS REACH IN—<u>SEIZING A PORTABLE
ROTARY SAW</u>—

INT. FALCONE'S LOFT—TV ROOM—SIMULTANEOUS

TV light flickers in Falcone's eyes as he gazes in shock:

FALCONE
...holy <u>shit</u>...

GC1 NEWSCASTER (O.S.)
...the recording was provided to
GC1 by Lieutenant James
Gordon of the Gotham PD—I
should warn you, the contents
are disturbing.

ON TV we see THE GC1 BREAKING NEWS HEADLINE—
"**<u>RECLUSIVE CRIME BOSS RECORDED COMMITTING</u>**
<u>MURDER</u>—**<u>ADMITS TO BEING MAFIA INFORMANT</u>**"—
SELINA'S CELLPHONE VOICEMAIL PLAYS—

FALCONE (ON TV)
—*ohhhh—he <u>told</u> you bout that,*
huh?—a <u>deal</u>—?

ANNIKA (ON TV)
—*yeah, long time ago he said—he*
said you gave some information
on some <u>drops thing</u>—

ON SELINA—IN THE DRAWING ROOM

WATCHING the two men by the TV, backs to her—<u>she slips</u>
<u>her hand into her clutch</u>—gripping **THE GLOCK**—<u>she RISES,</u>
<u>heading for them</u>—as ANNIKA **SCREAMS** <u>on TV</u>—!

INT. THE CLUB ELECTRICAL ROOM—SIMULTANEOUS

THE ROTARY SAW GRINDS INTO METAL AROUND POWER
LINES—**SPARKS FLY**—illuminating **THE BAT COWL IN**
THE DUFFLE!

INT. FALCONE'S LOFT—TV ROOM—SIMULTANEOUS

WE SLOWLY MOVE TOWARD THE BACK OF FALCONE'S HEAD—when the GLOCK lifts into frame—we hear a soft voice:

> SELINA (OS)
> ...hey, Dad...

Confused, Falcone turns to look at us, startled to see the gun—REVEAL SELINA, Glock in both hands, trained on Falcone—the Bald Bodyguard turns, alarmed too—

> FALCONE
> ...what...?

CLOSE ON SELINA, emotion under the stillness of her gaze:

> SELINA
> I'm Maria Kyle's kid...

Falcone looks at her, stunned, unnerved—then—

> FALCONE
> —OK, just—just put down the
> gun, honey—

> SELINA
> (cutting him off)
> —this is for my mother—

Selina about to fire—WHEN **THE LIGHTS GO OUT**—**AS BANG**—HER MUZZLE FLASH CATCHES THE BLUR OF FALCONE DUCKING—

INT. THE CLUB BELOW—IMMEDIATELY

CROWD reacting to the SUDDEN DARK in panic—

INSIDE THE ELEVATOR SHAFT

THE DOORS SCREECH OPEN—**A SHADOW** SWEEPS IN—as it passes, we see THE ELEVATOR GUARD outside, UNCONSCIOUS—

FROM DIRECTLY OVERHEAD IN THE SHAFT

RIGHT BELOW US, **THE SHADOW** RAISES... **THE GRAPPLING GUN**—THE **HOOK SOARS** TO THE ELEVATOR CAR, five stories above—

INT. FALCONE'S DARKENED TV ROOM UPSTAIRS— SIMULTANEOUS

SILHOUETTED AGAINST THE WINDOW, Selina and Bald Bodyguard FIGHT FOR HER GUN—SELINA SLAMS A HEEL ON HIS KNEE—HOBBLING him with a SICKENING CRACK—she SPINS—a BLINDING ROUNDHOUSE—and he DROPS—SELINA SPOTS—**A DIM GLIMPSE OF FALCONE DARTING FOR THE DOOR**—SHE FIRES BLINDLY— BULLETS RIPPING INTO THE WALL—WHILE—

OUTSIDE IN THE COMPLETELY DARKENED ELEVATOR HALLWAY

VOICES OF PANICKED GUARDS react to the GUN SHOTS—

> ONE GUARD (OS)
> Jesus Christ—!

ANOTHER (OS)
—I can't see a goddamn—

YET ANOTHER
—here-here-here—!

—as he turns on a CELL PHONE FLASHLIGHT—light spills onto THE FIVE ARMED GUARDS—WHEN AN OMINOUS SCREECHING comes from the end of the hall—THEY ALL SPIN toward—

THE EERILY OPEN DOORS OF THE PITCH-DARK ELEVATOR. They exchange looks, spooked; then, drawing guns, nod to the Guard With The Cell to check it out; he reluctantly moves to the doors, drawing his gun... they watch as he enters:

THE ELEVATOR

SCOURING with the GLOW of his cell; sees nothing... when, he hears BREATHING... dawning dread... he looks up AT—

BATMAN, BRACED UNNATURALLY AGAINST THE CEILING—light from below DISTORTING HIS FEATURES—an IMAGE FROM CHILDREN'S NIGHTMARES—FACE TO FACE with the Guard—

BATMAN DROPS—THE GUARD SHRIEKING IN AGONY—HIS CELL SMASHING—THE HALL **THRUST AGAIN INTO DARKNESS**—**AS BOOTSTEPS POUND**—BATMAN'S PATH THROUGH THE HALL MARKED BY **STACCATO MUZZLE FLASHES**—AS HE **PUMMELS GUARD, AFTER GUARD,** WEAPONS FIRING INVOLUNTARILY AS THEIR **BODIES FLY**—

MORE FLASHES FROM SELINA'S GUN reveal—FALCONE
CRAWLING DESPERATELY around the pool table—BARELY
EVADING HER—SELINA TURNS THE CORNER TO FIND
HIM—<u>ABOUT TO FIRE</u>—

WHEN A FORCE YANKS HER—SLAMMING HER INTO THE
TABLE—<u>THE BALD BODYGUARD</u>—SHE KICKS HIM OFF—
AND WITH <u>ANOTHER BRUTAL STOMP HOBBLES HIS</u>
OTHER KNEE—SHE GRABS HIS HEAD—<u>WHACKING HIM
OUT ON THE TABLE EDGE</u>!

SELINA SPINS BACK for Falcone—<u>BUT HE'S GONE</u>—
THWACK!—<u>FALCONE SLAMS HER HEAD WITH A POOL
CUE</u>! CLIMBS ON HER AS SHE DROPS—THRUSTING THE
CUE IN BOTH HANDS AGAINST HER NECK, **CHOKING
HER**—SELINA GASPS—ARMS PINNED—WRITHING—**A
EERIE COLDNESS IN HIS EYES** AS HE FIGHTS TO SNUFF
OUT HER LIFE—**FURIOUS TEARS SPILL** FROM HER EYES—

> FALCONE
> You don't think this <u>hurts</u> me...?
> My own... flesh and blood? You
> made me do this... Just... like
> your mother...

WHEN A SHAPE LOOMS—**<u>RIPPING FALCONE OFF</u>! IT'S
BATMAN**—SHOCKED, SELINA DRINKS IN AIR—<u>AS
BATMAN **SLAMS FALCONE** DOWN ONTO THE TABLE—
LEAVING HIM IN A STUPID DAZE</u>—Selina GRABS THE
GUN—aiming at Falcone—distraught, filled with fury—
Batman holds her back—she ERUPTS:

> SELINA
> <u>He has to PAY</u>—!

Batman gently puts his hand on the gun—as she shakes, still panting, adrenaline surging—he says, quietly:

> BATMAN
> But you shouldn't have to pay
> with him...

She turns to him—not understanding—still frenzied—

> BATMAN
> ...you've paid enough.

Something in that finally gets through... she relents... Batman watches as her eyes drift down, lost, reeling...

INT. ICEBERG LOUNGE—LONG ENTRY HALL—MOMENTS LATER

ONLOOKERS part—A STUNNED PENGUIN AND TWINS AMONG THEM—as Batman propels Falcone... who murmurs, undeterred—

> FALCONE
> Jesus, lookit you... Whattaya
> think this is—you think you're
> gonna scare me with that mask
> and the cape—I'm gonna start
> cryin' and some big secret's
> comin' out?

Batman slowly turns, rage now smoldering in his eyes.

> FALCONE
> Lemme tell you something:
> whatever I know, whatever I
> done, it's all goin' with me, OK?
> To my grave.

Batman gazes into his black eyes, restraining himself—then turns to see—GORDON waiting with a SHOTGUN at the open front door—Falcone smirks as they reach him—

> FALCONE
> You with Zorro over here?
>
> (leans in, hushed)
> Don't you know you boys in blue
> work for me...?

Gordon just glares, as he and Batman both shove Falcone—

OUTSIDE THE CLUB

where Falcone's smile immediately fades as he sees a HUGE DISPLAY OF ARMED COPS waiting in stoic silence—

> GORDON
> Guess we don't all work for you.

Falcone's stunned; Gordon nods to Martinez to CUFF him—

> GORDON
> You have the right to remain
> silent, anything you say can and
> will be used against you...

Falcone's eyes drift to Penguin and Twins who've emerged with others from the club, all watching in disgust—

> PENGUIN
> ...goddamn rat...
>
> FALCONE
> —what'd you say...?!

PENGUIN

Enjoy your night at Blackgate,
Carmine—probably be your
last—

FALCONE

Oh, you're a big man now, huh
Oz?

PENGUIN
(new sense of power)
—maybe I am—

FALCONE

Really, Oz? 'Cuz to me you were
always just a gimp in an empty
suit...

—the Twins can't help but chuckle at that—the public
humiliation suddenly embarrassing Penguin—he explodes:

PENGUIN

I'LL SPRAY-PAINT YOUR ASS—!

—whipping out his UZI—COPS FREAK—RUSHING HIM—
WHEN **SHOTS RING OUT**—**FALCONE'S HIT**—THE COPS
PILE ONTO PENGUIN—WHO SUBMITS IN SUDDEN PANIC—

PENGUIN

I DIDN'T SHOOT—I DIDN'T
SHOOT!

PANDEMONIUM—EVERYONE SCRAMBLING FOR
COVER—AS **BATMAN LOOKS UP** TO SEE—**A RIFLE**
JUTTING OUT A SIXTH-FLOOR WINDOW ACROSS THE
STREET—HE LUNGES FOR FALCONE—AS THE **RIFLE**

FIRES AGAIN—BULLETS EXPLODE INTO FALCONE'S CHEST—AS BATMAN TACKLES HIM—THEY TUMBLE TO THE GROUND—

AND THE **GUNFIRE FINALLY STOPS**—Batman rolls off Falcone—to find him BLEEDING OUT—when HE NOTICES **A BRIGHT REFLECTION** in the POOLING BLOOD—he looks up to see it's from the **LONE FLICKERING STREET LAMP** above—when SOMETHING QUIETLY DAWNS—

> BATMAN
> ...*"Bring him into the light..."*

His HEAD WHIPS to the DARKENED WINDOW ACROSS THE STREET—

> BATMAN
> *"...and you'll find where I'm—"*

> A VOICE CRIES (OS)
> (as if completing Batman's thought)
> UP THERE!

Everyone turns to see MARTINEZ POINTING TO THE WINDOW—

> MARTINEZ
> —THE SHOTS CAME FROM UP
> THERE!

—cops pulling out weapons—Batman turning to Gordon—

> BATMAN
> —it's Riddler—

Gordon struck, snapping into action—CALLING HIS MEN—

GORDON
Gage! On me! Martinez! Round
back! NO ONE GETS IN OR
OUTTA THERE!

COPS RUSH THE BUILDING—as Batman stalks purposefully alone in the direction of the window itself—

A few cops remain, attending to Falcone—HIS FACE GOES STILL—when A SHADOW SPILLS over his lifeless eyes—REVEAL SELINA above him—flickering street light flaring around her as she stares at her father, numb...

SMASH TO:

A GRAPPLING HOOK CRASHES THROUGH A WINDOW—
BATMAN CATAPULTS UP INTO—

<u>A RUN-DOWN STUDIO APARTMENT</u>

<u>NO ONE HERE</u>. The WALLS are COVERED IN IMAGES. Batman sees <u>A SNIPER RIFLE by the window</u>. He turns to AN OPEN WINDOW on another wall—moves to find—<u>A FIRE ESCAPE OUTSIDE</u>—leans to scan the grimy alley below—it's <u>EMPTY</u>—

THE FRONT DOOR SMASHES IN—Gordon and cops charge in—

> BATMAN
>> He's gone—

Batman moves past CAGES OF SCREECHING RATS to photos on the wall—Savage and the dealer—Mitchell and Annika—struck, Batman gazes out the window—Gordon does too—to SEE <u>most of the photos were taken from this spot</u>—

> GORDON
>> ...<u>he's been here this whole time?</u>

> MARTINEZ (OVER RADIO)
>> <u>LIEUTENANT</u>! We gotta witness here says she saw someone come down the fire escape right after the shots! She said he went into the corner diner—<u>the guy's sitting by himself at the counter right now</u>!

<u>Gordon and Batman exchange a look</u>...

EXT. PUSHING IN ON THE FRONT OF A LONELY DINER—NIGHT

Like an Edward Hopper painting—A LONE, AVERAGE-SIZED MAN sits at the counter, HIS BACK TO THE LARGE

WINDOW—A COUNTERMAN sets A LATTE before him, then disappears into the kitchen—a TV above plays ELECTION RESULTS—as we PUSH CLOSER—ARMED COPS CREEP INTO FRAME—

AMONG THE COPS—<u>WE FIND BATMAN</u>—as he approaches—staring at the Lone Man in the window—transfixed—

INT. LONELY CORNER DINER—THE COUNTER—SIMULTANEOUS

CLOSE ON THE BACK OF THE LONE MAN as he meticulously attends to HIS LATTE with a PLASTIC STIRRER; we HEAR—

> **GC1 NEWSCASTER**
> —not enough precincts in to call yet, but so far Reál is ahead of Acting Mayor Tomlin by huge margins, celebrations already beginning at her headquarters in Gotham Square Garden where even Don Mitchell's wife and son have gathered to show unity—

> **A CRAZED COP (OS)**
> <u>POLICE!!!—HANDS UP!</u>!!

<u>BUT THE LONE MAN JUST KEEPS STIRRING HIS LATTE</u>—

> **A CRAZED COP (OS)**
> I SAID PUT YOUR **GODDAMN HANDS UP**, YOU **SONUVABITCH**!!!

The Man FINISHES STIRRING... SLOWLY RAISES HIS HANDS, <u>still pinching the little stirrer</u>... He starts to turn—<u>but before we see his face</u>—REVEAL—<u>the SHOW OF FORCE AROUND HIM</u>—<u>THE PLACE IS PACKED</u>—

Then, at last, WE SEE **HIM** FOR THE FIRST TIME—and **his signature PRESCRIPTION AVIATORS**; he's pale, unremarkable; **a NOBODY**. A creepy half-smile forms as he stares at the cops—like he's been <u>expecting</u> them... when finally, he speaks, gesturing toward the kitchen with the stirrer—

> RIDDLER
> (as if they'll wait)
> ...I just ordered a slice of the
> pumpkin pie—

BAM!—COPS RUSH HIM—SLAMMING HIM ONTO THE COUNTER—

CLOSE ON HIS SIDEWAYS FACE, cheek pressed flat beside HIS LATTE—glasses smashed—<u>STRUCK, AS HE SEES SOMETHING</u>—past the cops, a FIGURE gazes from outside—**BATMAN**—RIDDLER holds Batman's eyes, smile growing—when Martinez rips his wallet from his pocket—<u>finding TWO DRIVER'S LICENSES</u>: "EDWARD NASHTON" and "PATRICK PARKER".

> MARTINEZ
> Which one is you?!

> RIDDLER
> (a little grin)
> ...you tell me...

> MARTINEZ
> Awright—<u>let's go, pencil-neck</u>!

As THEY TEAR HIM AWAY, we REMAIN ON HIS STEAMING LATTE—MOVING TOWARD THE CUP—LIFTING TO LOOK

INSIDE at what Riddler was working on—<u>A WORK OF LATTE</u> <u>ART</u>—**<u>A WHITE QUESTION MARK, SCRAWLED IN</u>** **<u>FOAM</u>**—HOLD, as SIRENS wail—

INT. RIDDLER'S STUDIO APARTMENT—SHORT TIME LATER

Crawling with INVESTIGATORS—POLICE PHOTOGRAPERS snap and videotape—the atmosphere is hushed, <u>electric</u>—

IN THE DIM HALLWAY RIGHT OUTSIDE

Martinez posted at the door, watches election results on his phone—when a DARK SHADOW WIPES RIGHT BY him—

Martinez just catches it—too late—

> MARTINEZ
> <u>Hey</u>—!

INSIDE THE APARTMENT

We ROVE toward DETECTIVES poring over a mountain of RIDDLER'S NOTEBOOKS, LEDGERS, PAPERS—so absorbed in their task they don't notice as we arrive beside them—

REVEAL BATMAN—scanning SCRIBBLED TITLES on the ledgers—he cocks his head to read one, struck: "**<u>RENEWAL</u>**"

On the other side of the room, Gordon confers with a FORENSIC COP by a PILE OF YELLOWING, RATTY NOTEBOOKS—

> GORDON
> —what <u>are</u> all these—<u>diaries</u>?

FORENSIC COP
Ledgers—he's got thousands—
scrawled all over 'em—
ramblings—ciphers—codes—

A DETECTIVE ON THE PHONE suddenly shouts excitedly—

DETECTIVE ON THE PHONE
Got something back on one of
the I.D.s! Edward Nashton!
Works at KTMJ! He's a forensic
accountant!

GORDON
—accountant—?

A SURLY COP YELLS (OS)
Hey, lieutenant! You really OK
with this—?!

Gordon turns—to see the Surly Cop gesturing beside Batman
who's now reading the Renewal ledger—

SURLY COP
What about chain of evidence?

Ignoring him, Batman looks up at Gordon with a foreboding
stare—Gordon approaches; Batman hands him the ledger—

GORDON
(shrugs to Surly Cop)
...he's wearing gloves...

Gordon gazes at the ledger—the top sheet is smothered in
WRITING, SCRAWLED right on the columns of numbers—as
GORDON READS—we **SEE** Batman stalk the room, absorbing

the **CLUTTER**—including a SHRINE OF MANNEQUINS WEARING PROTOTYPES OF THE RIDDLER'S TORTURE DEVICES...

> GORDON (OS)
>
> *"Friday, July, 16th. My life has been a cruel riddle I could not solve, suffocating my mind, no escape. But then today, I SAW IT... A SINGLE WORD on this ledger, sitting on the desk beside me! RENEWAL! The empty promise they sold to me as a child in that orphanage. One look inside and finally I UNDERSTOOD! My whole life has been PREPARING me for this... The moment when I would learn the TRUTH... when I could finally strike back and EXPOSE THEIR LIES!"*

As Batman passes CAGES OF AGITATED RATS, a **SCREECHING** grabs his attention; he moves for it as Gordon goes on—

> GORDON (OS)
>
> *"If you want people to understand, REALLY understand, you can't just give them the answers. You have to CONFRONT them, TORTURE THEM with the horrifying questions—just like they tortured ME. I KNOW NOW WHAT I MUST BECOME."*

As the **SCREECHING ESCALATES**, Gordon flips more pages, the Riddler's scrawl becoming illegible, until it's nothing but ANGRY SCARS OF INK—Gordon is shaken by the display of insanity—until the intense **SCREECHING** becomes TOO MUCH—he glances up, seeing Batman by the cages—

> GORDON
> Jesus—I don't think that rat likes
> you, man—

> BATMAN
> This one's not a rat...

Gordon and the Surly Cop step closer to see... inside the cage is **A RABID BAT**! It SNARLS, BEARING ITS TEETH, WINGS BEATING—beneath it is an ENVELOPE: "**TO THE BATMAN**"—attached to a strange **BLOODY, METAL TOOL**—

> GORDON
> What is that...?

Batman starts to reach in—but stops, shooting Surly Cop a sardonic look—okay with you?

> SURLY COP
> Knock yourself out...

As a Photographer FLASHES the cage, the bat HISSES MADLY—Batman tensely reaches past it, carefully retrieving the envelope and metal object—

> FORENSIC DETECTIVE
> Some kinda pry tool—

                    SURLY COP
            —is it a <u>chisel</u>—?

                     BATMAN
            —<u>it's a murder weapon</u>. He
            killed Mitchell with it.

                  (off their looks)
            The edge'll match the floorboard
            impression in the mayor's
            study.

Batman opens the envelope—another GREETING CARD
says: "JUST FOR YOU"; inside is SCRAWLED, "**MY**
CONFESSION..."

                     GORDON
            "<u>My Confession</u>"...? What's he
            <u>confessing</u> to? He already <u>told</u> us
            he killed Mitchell...

Batman stares at the card with growing dread—

                     BATMAN
            <u>This isn't over</u>...

               AN ALARMED VOICE (OS)
            Oh man—he's been posting all
            kinds of shit online! He's got like
            <u>five hundred followers</u>—<u>real</u>
            <u>fringe types</u>...

They turn to a DIGITAL FORENSICS COP on Riddler's laptop—
Gordon moves to see—but Batman's eyes go to the wall above...
to **AN ENORMOUS COLLAGE**—a sea of DEFACED PHOTOS—
scrawled over it: "**<u>THE TRUTH ABOUT GOTHAM</u>**".

Batman steps forward, gazing at IMAGES of city officials, police officers, Riddler's victims—but most prominent is an image of YOUNG BRUCE WAYNE beside his father at the Orphanage ceremony—their **EYES ETCHED ANGRILY OUT**.

In the BOY'S CHOIR beside them, a QUESTION MARK encircles the head of a SAD, SCRAWNY BOY IN AVIATOR GLASSES who stares at the Waynes in awe—next to him are the words: **"If only I knew then... what I KNOW now..."**—

—Batman sees A CLUSTER OF BATMAN TABLOID HEADLINES in the collage—among them, a CRUDE POLICE SKETCH, entitled: **"GOTHAM TERRORIZED—WHO IS THE BATMAN?"** Next to it, Riddler has written ominously: **"I KNOW... I know the REAL you..."** Batman stares, unnerved—WHEN—

> DIGITAL FORENSICS COP (OS)
> His final post was last night—
> some video—gotta lotta views—
> but it's password protected—

Batman turns to see what they're looking at—the post is titled **"The Truth UNMASKED"**—Batman hit by a sinking feeling as Gordon anxiously presses toward the screen—

> GORDON
> Can you get in—?

> DIGITAL FORENSICS COP
> Copying his drive now—take
> some time—but we'll get in...

Batman stares, world closing in—reeling—then—

> BATMAN
> I think I'm his last target...

Gordon turns—struck—

> GORDON
> You...?

> BATMAN
> Maybe this's all coming to an
> end.

> GORDON
> ...what is?

> BATMAN
> The Batman.

Gordon looks confused, when his phone RINGS. He steps
away. Batman watches as Gordon speaks low—his eyes
suddenly lift darkly to Batman's. He hangs up, unnerved—

> GORDON
> ...Riddler's asking for you. At
> Arkham.

Batman just looks at him; then starts to go—but stops—
Gordon looks at him—when he says, like a farewell—

> BATMAN
> ...you're a good cop.

**INT. VISITING CELL—ARKHAM PRISON FOR THE INSANE—
NIGHT**

Batman waits as the METAL ROLL-UP DOOR RISES...
revealing Riddler. Seeing Batman, an EERIE SMILE grows.
Finally, Riddler speaks, glancing at the squalid
surroundings—

> RIDDLER
> ...I told you I'd see you in hell.

> BATMAN
> What do you want from me?

> RIDDLER
> ...want? If you only knew how
> long I've been waiting for this
> day... for this moment. I've been
> invisible my whole life. Guess I
> won't be anymore, will I? They'll
> remember me now. They'll
> remember both of us...

His smile fades. He looks into Batman's eyes; ominously:

> RIDDLER
> Bruce Wayne...

Batman's jaw clenches, betraying nothing—Riddler's emotion
rises, he looks at the floor, stewing with rage:

> RIDDLER
> Bruce. Waaaayne.

Batman on edge—his eyes flit anxiously to a SECURITY
CAMERA recording—when Riddler's eyes snap back to his.
The pause between them is excruciating. Then, bitterly:

RIDDLER

You know, I was there that day...
the day the great Thomas Wayne
announced he was running
for mayor. Made all those
promises... Week later he was
dead, and everybody just forgot
about us. All they could talk
about was <u>poor Bruce Wayne</u>...
Bruce Wayne the orphan...
<u>Orphan</u>? Living in some tower
over the park isn't being an
orphan. Looking down at
everyone with all that money—

don't you tell _me_... You know
what being an orphan is? Thirty
kids to a room, twelve years
old and already a drophead,
numbing the pain—you wake up
screaming with rats chewing
your fingers, and every winter
one of the babies dies because
it's so cold. But oh, no. Let's focus
on the billionaire with the lying
dead daddy. Because at least the
money makes it go down easy,
doesn't it?

(glaring at Batman)
Bruce Wayne...

Riddler quiets, ruminating darkly. Walls closing in, Batman
looks away to keep from screaming. Riddler sighs:

RIDDLER
He's the only one we didn't get.

Batman lifts his eyes—stirring almost imperceptibly—what'd
he just say? Riddler leans in conspiratorially—

RIDDLER
But we got the rest of them,
didn't we—all those sick, sleazy,
phony pricks...

Batman REELS—**Riddler DOESN'T know**—when, Riddler
suddenly softens, his tone turning almost vulnerable:

RIDDLER
God, look at you... Your... mask

is amazing. I wish you could have seen me in mine...

(an intimate grin)

Isn't it funny? All everyone wants to do is unmask you, but they're missing the point... You and I both know: I'm looking at the <u>real</u> you right now. My mask allowed me to be myself, completely. No shame. No limits—

BATMAN

—<u>why did you write me</u>?

RIDDLER

......what do you mean?

BATMAN

<u>All those cards</u>—

RIDDLER

I <u>told</u> you. We've been doing this <u>together</u>—you're <u>part</u> of this—

BATMAN

<u>We didn't do anything together</u>—

RIDDLER

—we <u>did</u>—what did we just do? I asked you to bring him into the light and <u>you did</u>—we're such a <u>good team</u>—

BATMAN

We're NOT a team—

RIDDLER

I never could have gotten him out of there, I'm not—physical— my strength is up here. I mean I had all the pieces, I had the answers, but I didn't know how to make them listen—YOU gave me that—

BATMAN

I gave you NOTHING—

RIDDLER

—you showed me what was possible—you showed me all it takes is fear and a little focused violence—you INSPIRED me—

BATMAN

YOU'RE OUT OF YOUR GODDAMN MIND!

RIDDLER

What—?

BATMAN

—this is all in your HEAD— you're twisted—SICK—

RIDDLER

—how can you say that?!

> BATMAN
> —you think you'll be
> REMEMBERED? You're a
> pathetic psychopath begging for
> attention—you're gonna die in
> Arkham—FORGOTTEN—a
> NOBODY—!

> RIDDLER
> —no—no—stop—!

(covering his ears, a child's tantrum)
NO, NO, NO, NO, NO, NO—
AHHHHHHHHHHHHHHHH—

> RIDDLER
> (angry tears stream)
> **—THIS IS NOT HOW THIS**
> **WAS SUPPOSED TO GO**...!!!

SILENCE. Batman watches Riddler fume to himself; quietly:

> RIDDLER
> I had it all planned out. We were
> gonna be safe here—we could
> watch the whole thing.
> Together.

> BATMAN
> ...watch what?

> RIDDLER
> (sulking at floor)
> Everything. But I guess that
> won't be happening now, will it?

He glares up at Batman... and suddenly registers <u>Batman has no idea what he's talking about</u>. Riddler's struck—

> RIDDLER
> ...<u>ohhhh</u>... you didn't—?—it was <u>all there</u>... you didn't figure it <u>out</u>...?
>
> (relishing)
> You're really not as <u>smart</u>... as I <u>thought</u> you were... I guess I gave you too much credit...

> BATMAN
> <u>What have you done?</u>

Riddler sits there; he leans in with sadistic pleasure—

> RIDDLER
> What's black and blue... <u>and dead all over</u>...?
>
> (as Batman glares)
> <u>You</u>. If you think you can stop what's coming...

> BATMAN
> <u>What have you DONE?!</u>

Riddler sinks silently into his chair, finally retreating into an eerie, off-key **"AVE MARIA"** by SHUBERT... BATMAN LAUNCHES out of his chair, SMASHING A FIST against the glass; but Riddler keeps singing. Batman stands, helpless— <u>STRAINS OF "AVE MARIA" RISING HAUNTINGLY</u>—

INT. RIDDLER'S DARKENED APARTMENT—FRONT DOOR—NIGHT

A BLADE SLASHES the POLICE SEAL on the door—BATMAN BUSTS IN, PLAGUED, folding his TACTICAL KNIFE—his eyes rove the unoccupied space—poring over the details again— WHAT DID HE MISS?—mind racing—WHEN—

> **A VOICE (OS)**
> Hey—whattaya doin' in here—?

Batman spins to see MARTINEZ IN THE DOORWAY, hand on his gun. No time for this, Batman shoots a terrifying look. Intimidated, Martinez thinks twice, releases his grip.

As Batman resumes his search, Martinez steps in, feeling a responsibility to monitor the situation... He watches as Batman moves to the BLOODY METAL TOOL, taking out his UV light bar, shining it. He picks up the GREETING CARD—

> **MARTINEZ**
> Hey man—I don't think you
> should be touching th—

Another look cuts him off—Batman studies the card. Martinez glances at the tool, attempting conversation—

> **MARTINEZ**
> ...boy, this guy's a real nutjob,
> huh? Killing Mitchell with a
> friggin' carpet tool...

Batman slowly turns, **struck**. He gives Martinez a crazed look: **what did you just say?** Martinez smiles, sheepish—

> **MARTINEZ**
> ...my uncle's an installer—it's a,
> it's a—you know—a tucker.

THE TOOL IS THE MISSING PIECE. Batman picks it up, stunned. Looks around frantically, finally spotting... a SUSPICIOUS, SNARLED CORNER OF THE RUG. He puts the tool down—moving toward the snag—Martinez watching— as he crouches to examine... when... with growing dread... he begins TUGGING UP THE RUG—CARPET TACKS **POP-POP-POP**! Martinez freaks as EVIDENCE ON THE RUG SPILLS CHAOTCALLY:

> MARTINEZ
> —whoa-WHOA-WHATTAYA **DOIN', MAN**?!

Batman UNVEILS A GIANT **MAP OF GOTHAM**, SCRAWLED ONTO THE FLOOR—it's INCREDIBLY DETAILED. Beside the map are frighteningly carved, huge words: "**A REAL CHANGE**"—Batman STARES at the WORDS, GEARS TURNING—he lifts his head—looking at SOMETHING across the room—

RIDDLER'S LAPTOP SCREEN—SECONDS LATER

Batman enters the words, "A REAL CHANGE"—unlocking the VIDEO... Riddler in his hooded uniform—his warm tone weirdly incongruous with the ominous VOICE CHANGER:

> RIDDLER (ON LAPTOP)
> *Hey guys, thanks for all the*
> *comments, and a special thanks*
> *to everyone for the tips on*
> *detonators. I just want to say...*
> *this will be my last post for a*
> *while, and, uh...*

(a surge of emotion)
...what this community has
meant to me... these weeks, these
months... let's just say... <u>none</u> of
us... is alone anymore, mm-k?

Batman stares—as Riddler tamps his feelings down—

RIDDLER (ON LAPTOP)
Tomorrow's election day, and
Bella Reál will win. She promised
<u>real change</u>. But we know the
<u>truth</u>, don't we? You've seen
Gotham's true face now. Together,
we've unmasked it. Its corruption,
its perversion, masquerading
under the guise of Renewal... but
unmasking is not enough... The
Day of Judgement is finally upon
us, and now it is time... <u>for</u>
<u>retribution</u>.

Riddler PICKS THE CAMERA UP, POINTS it at the MAP ON
THE FLOOR as he walks; <u>Batman RISES to FOLLOW THE</u>
<u>SAME PATH</u>—

RIDDLER (VO)
I've parked seven vans all along
the city sea wall. And on the big
night, they will... go... boom—

Batman gazes down, <u>SEES **SEVEN Xs** CARVED INTO</u>
<u>THE MAP</u>—

                    RIDDLER (VO)
          Now when things go wrong, cities
          have a _plan_. But tomorrow, we
          will turn it on its head. Make their
          *emergency disaster plan _truly a_*
          disaster. When the vans blow—

ALARMED, BATMAN PEERS DOWN at the X on a GOTHAM
STREET right under his feet—ALMOST GASPING—AS WE—

                                        MATCH CUT TO:
SAME ANGLE—OVER THE **ACTUAL** GOTHAM STREET—
THAT MOMENT

In the X's place is a VAN—as it **ERUPTS**, PART OF THE
ADJACENT SEA WALL CRUMBLING—**A RUSH OF WATER
FLOODS IN**!

BACK TO BATMAN

SPINNING at the sound of MORE EXPLOSIONS; he bolts to
the window to **SEE FIREBALLS ROILING OVER THE
SKYLINE**—!

                    RIDDLER (VO)
          —the flooding will happen so fast,
          evacuation will not be an option...

**NEW DISTANT ANGLE ON THE RISING FIREBALLS—
CONTINUOUS**

REVEAL RIDDLER peering out his cell window; he smiles—

**HIGH ANGLE—OVER ANOTHER GOTHAM STREET—AT THAT
MOMENT**

A STARTLING GLIMPSE—**A TSUNAMI WAVE** SWEEPS

SUDDENLY OVER SHOCKED PEDESTRIANS—TEARING THE STREET APART—

> RIDDLER (VO)
> *Those who are not washed*
> *away—*

RIDDLER'S APARTMENT—AT THAT MOMENT

Batman's head whips toward ANOTHER SCRAWLED INTER-SECTION—drawn by the sounds of DISTANT, **TERRIFIED SCREAMING**—it's as if the sound is coming from the map—

> RIDDLER (VO)
> *—will race through the streets in*
> *terror...*

SAME ANGLE ON THE ACTUAL INTERSECTION—AT THAT MOMENT

—THE DESTRUCTIVE WAVE—NOW BLACK WITH DEBRIS—RIPS UP CARS, TREES, LAMP POSTS—as PEOPLE'S **SCREAMS ECHO**—

BATMAN'S EYES

fiercely search the map—assessing the crisis—

> BATMAN
> Call Gordon—

> MARTINEZ
> (fumbling for cell)
> —yeah-yeah-yeah—!

> SMASH TO:

STREET OUTSIDE GOTHAM SQUARE GARDEN—THAT VERY MOMENT

CELEBRATING CROWDS watching Bella's victory on JUMBOTRONS and CELLS—as EMERGENCY BULLETINS interrupt coverage—

>   RIDDLER (VO)
> *As breaking news hits higher*
> *ground at Gotham Square*
> *Garden, celebrations will turn to*
> *panic—*

People react—SCREAMING—some spot SMOKE IN THE SKY—

>   RIDDLER (VO)
> *—as the venue becomes the city's*
> *shelter of last resort...*

BACK TO RIDDLER'S APARTMENT—AT THAT MOMENT

>   RIDDLER (ON LAPTOP)
> *And that's where all of **you** come*
> *in...*

BATMAN'S EYES GO TO THE COMMENT BOARD—finding CHILLING REPLIES: "**what gauge? what caliber?**"—"**rifles are good**"

>   RIDDLER (ON LAPTOP)
> *...when the time arrives, I will*
> *already be unmasked, the pigs*
> *will have me in their custody—but*
> *that's OK, because then... it will be*
> ***your** turn...*

SMASH TO:

A MOVING SHOT—FOLLOWING A DARK FIGURE

Walking THE RAFTERS ABOVE GOTHAM SQUARE GARDEN, <u>pulling on a **Riddler-style execution hood, rifle** in hand</u>...

> RIDDLER (VO)
> ...*you'll be there, waiting*...

The Hooded Figure stares ominously below where panicked commotion suggests news of the flooding is spreading—<u>when the Figure looks up, SPOTTING</u>...

<u>ANOTHER ARMED HOODED FIGURE</u>, staring back at him— they regard each other oddly... then nod grimly—when they turn to see... <u>a THIRD Riddler Figure arriving</u>... and behind him, <u>ANOTHER</u>... and <u>ANOTHER</u>... It's <u>A SMALL ARMY OF BITTER NOBODIES IN HOODED RIDDLER OUTFITS, hidden above the crowd, all meeting here for the very first time, as they secretly prepare to strike</u>...

> RIDDLER (VO)
> *It's time for the lies to finally*
> *end—false promises of Renewal,*
> *change—*

BACK TO BATMAN

watching in horror as Riddler concludes bitterly—

> RIDDLER (ON LAPTOP)
> <u>*We'll give them a **real**, real*</u>
> <u>*change now*</u>. *We've spent our lives*
> *in this wretched place, suffering,*
> *wondering why <u>us</u>? Now they will*
> *spend their last moments*

wondering, why __them__...?

ON MARTINEZ, completely terrified, gazing at his cell—

> MARTINEZ
> I can't get through—the lines are
> down—!

He turns to show Batman—**BUT BATMAN IS ALREADY GONE!**

EXT. OUTSIDE GOTHAM SQUARE GARDEN—NIGHT

UTTER CHAOS OUTSIDE THE GLASS DOMED BUILDING—
EMERGENCY VEHICLES, SIRENS—PEOPLE running up the
streets—FIRST RESPONDERS scream to CROWDS OF
TERRIFIED CITIZENS—herding them to shelter inside the
Garden—tending to the INJURED—a crisis escalating by the
second—

We SPOT a MOTORCYCLE weaving through the madness—
SELINA—with her leather backpack, saddle bags on the
bike—she stops at a ROAD BLOCK across the intersection—
hops off to move a SAW HORSE herself—WHEN:

> TRAFFIC COP
> Hey—road's CLOSED!

> SELINA
> —I'm trying to get outta __town__—

> TRAFFIC COP
> Lady, we got BOMBS goin' off,
> whole city's FLOODING! Now
> you're gonna have to go inside

the Garden with everyone else!

About to protest, Selina suddenly feels something—she looks down to see BLACK WATER POOLING around her feet—

INSIDE GOTHAM SQUARE GARDEN—ENTRANCE— SIMULTANEOUS

The victory celebration turned to crisis mode—a MAD CRUSH squeezes through the doors—fighting through, we FIND GORDON, rousted from bed, urgently heading for—a MAKESHIFT COMMAND POST. UNIFORMED OFFICERS, MED PERSONNEL and FIREMEN all talk at once; Gordon flashes his BADGE—

> GORDON
> MCU—who's in charge—?!

> YOUNG OFFICER
> I really dunno, we're all just
> tryin'a get a handle here, sir!

> GORDON
> —we have an active situation—
> we need to sweep the building
> for explosives and get the
> mayor-elect outta here, now.
> Where is she—?

INT. GOTHAM SQUARE GARDEN—HIGH ABOVE—SAME

A RIFLE SCOPE PROWLS the panicked crowd… FINDING **GORDON AND COPS** pressing through; CROSSHAIRS follow ominously—then SWISH ACROSS TO FIND—**BELLA** behind the FESTOONED STAGE, surrounded by her team, peeking in and out of view as she gestures anxiously, arguing with a FIRE MARSHALL—

REVEAL A MAGNIFIED EYE—blinking eerily through the scope—as the scope lowers, and we see ONE OF THE HOODED GUNMEN lying on his stomach IN THE RAFTERS—

Satisfied with his position, he lowers his rifle, opens a PLASTIC AMMO CASE revealing A HUNDRED ROUNDS. He takes one, begins to load—as we DISCOVER—<u>OTHER GUNMEN preparing their weapons on the rafters behind him</u>!

DOWN BELOW—BEHIND THE SCAFFOLDING STAGE—SAME

Gordon and the cops arrive to find Bella mid-argument with the Fire Marshall—Gordon notices Mitchell's Wife and Ten-Year-Old Son standing nervously with the group—

> FIRE MARSHALL
> If we don't close the doors, we're gonna have a huge problem, <u>water's already starting to breach</u>!

> BELLA REÁL
> I thought this was the <u>shelter of last resort</u>—!

> FIRE MARSHALL
> —yeah—for a <u>hurricane</u>—not if <u>the whole sea wall comes down</u>!

> BELLA REÁL
> —<u>I am not going to let those people die out there</u>!

(angry, distraught)
Awright... I'll go calm the crowd
down so we can get everyone in—

GORDON (OS)
—it's not safe for you here—

Bella turns—seeing Gordon and the cops—

GORDON
—we gotta get you out, Ms. Reál.

BELLA REÁL
I'm not going anywhere—

GORDON
—we are under attack—

BELLA REÁL
Exactly! That's the problem with
this city—everyone's afraid to
stand up and do the right thing.
But I'm not. Excuse me—

Gordon watches, frustrated, as she moves to the podium—

BELLA REÁL
Everyone!? Everyone! If I could
just get your attention—!

The unruly crowd won't quiet—she starts to call out again—
when, in the corner of her eye, she SPOTS—

THE **GLINT** OF A RIFLE up behind the lights—she recoils—
Gordon suddenly reading her fear—STARTING FOR HER
AS—**BANG! GUNFIRE ERUPTS** FROM THE RAFTERS!

BELLA DROPS AS SHE'S HIT—GORDON LAUNCHING TO SHIELD HER—**PANDEMONIUM**—AS **MORE SHOTS** RING OUT FROM ABOVE—GORDON FRANTICALLY DRAGS BELLA INTO COVER OFF-STAGE—

HE DRAWS HIS GUN—PEEKING AT THE RAFTERS—AS **A TORRENT OF MUZZLE FLASHES EXPLODES—THE GUNMEN FIRING!**

GORDON PEERS THROUGH THE SCAFFOLDING AT **WAVES OF PEOPLE** SCREAMING IN PANIC—THE SCENE RATCHETING INTO UNBEARABLE TENSION—GORDON HORRIFIED—WHEN SUDDENLY—

EXPLOSIONS RIP PERCUSSIVELY THROUGH THE DOMED CEILING—UNLEASHING A HAIL OF GLASS OVER THE GUNMEN—AS—A **MALEFIC PHANTOM** PLUMMETS THROUGH THE ROOF—**BATMAN**!!!

HE SLAMS INTO THE RAFTERS BARELY IN CONTROL— **TRIGGERING HIS QUICK-DRAW SLIDER**—FIRING A HARPOON LINE INTO THE LEG OF THE SHOOTER ON THE BEAM ACROSS FROM HIM—THEN—**A SECOND SLIDER** ON HIS OTHER ARM—HARPOONING **ANOTHER**—

BATMAN **FLIPS BACK OFF THE CATWALK**—YANKING BOTH GUNMEN OFF THEIR BEAMS—COUNTER-BALANCING BATMAN AS HE SWINGS UNDER THE CATWALK AND BACK UP ONTO IT—THE **SHOOTERS DANGLING** BELOW—**THIS HAS ALL HAPPENED IN AN INSTANT**—

IN SHOCK, THE ARMY OF HOODED LOOKALIKES TURNS— **FIRING**—AS **BATMAN BOUNDS MADLY** THROUGH THEIR ASSAULT—**TAKING HITS**—HE **LEAPS OUT ACROSS**

BEAMS—WILDLY GRASPING ONE—CATAPULTING HIMSELF UP INTO—A GROUP OF SHOOTERS—

WITH BLINDING SPEED, **BATMAN ATTACKS**—SNAPPING BONES—POPPING KNEECAPS—HE SPOTS A **TERRIFIED GUNMAN** RELOADING—STARTS FOR HIM—SUDDENLY **PULLED OFF BALANCE**—BATMAN SPINS TO SEE TWO OF THE BLOODIED NOBODIES GRIPPING HIS CAPE— DESPERATELY TRYING TO HEAVE HIM DOWN INTO THE ABYSS BELOW—BATMAN TWISTS HARD—WINCHING THE CAPE—YANKING THE NOBODIES INTO A FLURRY OF KNOCKOUT BLOWS—

BATMAN SEES THE **TERRIFIED GUNMAN** LIFTING HIS WEAPON—SPINS TO SEE **ANOTHER SHOOTER**—ABOUT TO FIRE TOO—BATMAN DODGING AS—THE ROUNDS RIP INTO THE **TERRIFIED GUNMAN** INSTEAD—AS HE DROPS, THE **TERRIFIED GUNMAN** FIRES INVOLUNTARILY— BULLETS TEARING INTO **THE OTHER SHOOTER—BUT ONE SHOT SMACKS HARD OFF THE SIDE OF BATMAN'S COWL!**

SEEING HIM DAZED—THE REMAINING GUNMEN **UNLEASH A FIRESTORM**—RABIDLY BLASTING BATMAN— BATMAN FORCED TO RETREAT, SHIELDING HIMSELF— AS THEY **STALK AFTER HIM**—

DOWN BELOW ON THE STAGE

HUNDREDS SCRAMBLE—**GORDON** presses against panic to see BATMAN UNDER ATTACK; turns to the Fire Marshall and cops:

GORDON
Get me up there...!

They leap from the stage into DEEP WATER, WADING URGENTLY PAST SOMEONE in the crowd—**SELINA**— PEOPLE JOSTLE HER as she fights to glimpse Batman—she pulls herself onto the scaffolding tower by the stage to see— WORRIED...

BACK IN THE RAFTERS

BATMAN STUMBLES, COLLAPSING—AS THE GUNMEN SHOOT—HE SEES **FIRE EXTINGUISHERS** ON THE RAILING—RIPS **A STICKY CHARGE** FROM HIS BELT— SLAPS IT ON ONE—ROLLS IT AT THE SHOOTERS—DOES THE SAME TO ANOTHER—AND ANOTHER—**WHEN THE CHARGES ALL BLOW!**—HUGE CLOUDS ERUPT INTO THE AIR—**AS BATMAN EVAPORATES INTO THEIR WHITENESS**—

THE SHOOTERS ANXIOUSLY VENTURE INTO THE FOG— ONE PROBES BLINDLY WITH HIS RIFLE—WHEN **BATMAN** SEIZES THE BARREL—**HIS FINGER TASER ZAPS** THE METAL—THE **GUNMAN COLLAPSES**—

BATMAN CLUBS THE SHOOTERS ONE BY ONE WITH THE RIFLE—HE SPOTS ONE CRAWLING FOR A DUFFLE—GOES FOR HIM—AS THE GUNMAN LIFTS OUT A SHOTGUN— **FIRING INTO BATMAN'S CHEST! BATMAN CAREENS OFF THE CATWALK—BARELY CATCHING THE EDGE WITH ONE HAND**—GASPING FOR BREATH—TRYING TO PULL HIMSELF UP—BUT THE PAIN IS JUST TOO MUCH—

THE SHOTGUN SHOOTER RISES, HALF IN SHOCK—HANDS SHAKING AS HE RELOADS—LIMPING TO THE EDGE, WILD EYES PEERING FROM THE EXECUTIONER'S HOOD AT BATMAN, HANGING BELOW—

BATMAN LOOKS UP, HELPLESS—<u>TREMBLING, THE</u> <u>SHOOTER PUTS HIS GUN TO BATMAN'S COWL</u>—**FINGER ON THE TRIGGER**—WHEN—OUT OF NOWHERE—**A BLINDING KICK KNOCKS HIS GUN FREE**—IT FIRES INTO THE AIR—AS THE GUNMAN SPINS TO SEE—

SELINA!—LEAPING FROM THE SCAFFOLDING—SHE **HOOK-KICKS** HIS HEAD INTO THE RAILING—CATCHING HIM AS HE REELS—<u>RAMMING HIS FACE DOWN HARD</u> <u>AGAIN</u>—THE GUNMAN CRUMPLES—

Selina moves to Batman—losing his grip, fading—no time to lose, she leans down, grabs his arm—braces her heels on the railing—levering him slowly up—until she collapses on the catwalk, his body on top of hers.

She rolls him onto his back, gazing down, face close to his. He looks up, haunted, as if he doesn't see her as he struggles to breathe—when she notices HIS CHEST—<u>the blast has torn his</u> <u>armor, buckshot lodged in exposed skin</u>—<u>a lot of blood</u>—it's unclear how bad the wound is—he tries to sit up—she guides

him back down—growing emotional—cradling his face—
soothing—

SELINA

...it's OK... it's done now... it's
over.

Finally he submits—his eyes now seeing hers—holding
them—then, gently closing... Eyes welling, she leans down
to kiss his face... his lips... as she pulls back... his eyes open;
for a moment, they just stare—when—

—Batman sees A SHAPE looming above Selina—IT'S THE
BATTERED SHOTGUN SHOOTER—WHOSE FOOT SLAMS
THE BACK OF HER HEAD—STUNNING HER—HE DRAGS
HER OFF BATMAN—**UNSHEATHING A HUNTING KNIFE**
FROM HIS BOOT—SHE RAISES HER ARMS TO DEFEND
HERSELF—**AS HE STABS WILDLY AT HER!**

BATMAN FIGHTS TO GET UP—HE CAN'T—AS SELINA
STRUGGLES—HE FUMBLES SOMETHING FROM HIS BELT—
AN AUTO-INJECTOR: **ADRENALINE**—**HE JAMS IT INTO
HIS NECK!**

HE LAUNCHES HIMSELF WITH A JOLT—RIPPING THE
ATTACKER OFF SELINA IN **A VIOLENT FRENZY**—**LOSING
ALL CONTROL**—SELINA STUNNED BY BATMAN'S
UNBRIDLED PRIMAL RAGE—WHEN—**GORDON** AND THE
COPS BURST OUT A DOOR TO THE CATWALK—GORDON
RACES TO BATMAN—**TO STOP HIM FROM KILLING**—

GORDON

Hey man—take it easy—take it
easy—! Hey—**HEY**—!

Batman stops, mid-strike—Gordon's voice reaching him—he turns, disoriented, as Gordon gently pulls him back—Batman slowly stands, breathing hard—turns—checking on Selina— as she rises, looking at him, grateful, surprised, the depth of his feelings for her now exposed.

Gordon reaches down, pulling the Hood off the SHOOTER—

> **GORDON**
> Jesus... who the hell are you...?

> **UNKNOWN MAN**
> (grins eerily)
> Me...? **I'm Vengeance.**

Batman turns, struck by the sound of his own words in this killer's mouth—WHEN—A CRASH ECHOES BELOW—!

Everyone spins—EXCEPT BATMAN—who continues to stare at the Man, ROCKED—HOLD ON HIM as the **SOUNDS OF PANIC AND CHAOS FADE AWAY**—when FLICKERING LIGHTS in the arena pull him out of his trance—Batman turns to the others—**COMPLETE SILENCE** as DOWN BELOW he SEES—

THE FOUR-STORY GLASS WALL BEHIND THE STAGE SMASHING OPEN AS CASCADING DEBRIS FLOODS INSIDE—UPROOTED TREES, CARS, AND WAVES OF BLACK WATER SWARMING THE SCAFFOLDING AROUND THE STAGE—**WHICH GIVES WAY ALL AT ONCE**—

BATMAN AND THE OTHERS WATCH PEOPLE TOSSED INTO SWEEPING MUCK—SCAFFOLDING TOWERS TOPPLE, **SHEARING ELECTRICAL LINES** POWERING THE HUGE MONITORS AND LIGHTS—BATMAN SEES **ONE LINE**

SPARKING ANGRILY OVER THE RAPIDLY RISING WATER—**THE WIRE THREATENING TO MAKE CONTACT WITH THE SURFACE, JEOPARDIZING THE THOUSANDS HALF-SUBMERGED**—

GORDON, SELINA, AND THE COPS WATCH HELPLESSLY— BATMAN WITHDRAWS HIS GRAPPLE GUN—FIRING INTO THE CEILING—THEY TURN AGHAST AS HE SWINGS OUT— ONTO THE POWER LINE!

BATMAN PULLS HIS TACTICAL KNIFE—BRACING HIMSELF—**HE HACKS THE LINE**—SOUND COMES CRASHING BACK—**AS AN ELECTRICAL BLAST SURGES THROUGH HIM**—JOLTING HIM LOOSE—**HE DROPS TO THE WATER BELOW, SPLASHING INTO IT**! SELINA AND GORDON WATCH IN HORROR—**AS ALL THE LIGHTS GO OUT**—

FOR A MOMENT, WE WONDER: **IS BATMAN DEAD**? WHEN—HE BREAKS THE SURFACE, GASPING, ALIVE. Scans the darkness around him, pulling something from his belt; it IGNITES, and we see it's A FLARE—THE SOLE SOURCE OF LIGHT NOW ILLUMINATING THE THOUSANDS IN THE WATER ALL AROUND HIM—

He sees BELLA AND OTHERS, trapped in twisted scaffolding in the STILL-RISING WATER—he starts quickly toward them—climbs the wreckage—heaving a truss aside to make an opening to let them all out—but as he reaches in, Bella and the group hesitate, intimidated by Batman's haunting, wraith-like presence in the flare's light—all, except a **BOY**... **MITCHELL'S TEN-YEAR-OLD SON**, who reaches his hand up, unafraid. Batman pulls him up... He turns to Bella, offering a hand again... she takes it. As she clings to him, the others begin climbing out too—

NIRVANA'S "**SOMETHING IN THE WAY**" BEGINS—
as Batman uses **HIS FLARE AS A BEACON**, leading the
masses through water, everyone following to safety—
<u>**a mesmerizing sight**</u>...

> BRUCE (VO)
> Wednesday, November sixth...
> The city is underwater...

EXT. EXTREME HIGH AND WIDE OVER LOWER GOTHAM—
SUNRISE

Light fills the sky; <u>the island is COMPLETELY SUBMERGED</u>—

> BRUCE (VO)
> The national guard is coming...

EXT. LOWER GOTHAM STREETS—A SERIES OF SHOTS—
SUNRISE

REVISITING KEY LOCATIONS FROM OUR STORY—the FLOODED SCENES OF AFTERMATH appear serene, surreally beautiful... **WE SEE**—the half-sunk **CITY HALL**—facade ripped open—a lone dog paddles past the tops of traffic lights—

> BRUCE (VO)
> Martial law is in effect. But the
> criminal element never sleeps...

—**THE DINER** WHERE RIDDLER WAS CAUGHT—SUN GLEAMS IN ON A SMALL FLEET OF PYREX COFFEE POTS, WHICH FLOAT EERILY—

> BRUCE (VO)
> Looting and lawlessness will be
> rampant in the parts of the city
> no one can get to...

—THE ICEBERG LOUNGE—THE EMPTY DANCE FLOOR NOW SWIMMING IN STILL WATER UNDER SHIMMERING STAGE LIGHTS—

> BRUCE (VO)
> I can already see, things will get
> worse before they get better...

—**FALCONE'S DRAWING ROOM**—FRESH, WET FOOT PRINTS LEAD TO A LONE FIGURE SEATED IN FALCONE'S CHAIR; PENGUIN—

> BRUCE (VO)
> And some will seize the chance
> to grab everything they can...

—Penguin sips scotch from Falcone's crystal tumbler, staring out over the city, his mind turning darkly...

EXT. GOTHAM HOSPITAL TRIAGE CENTER—SUNRISE

In bandages, BELLA REÁL holds a PRESS CONFERENCE;
GORDON among the embattled POLICE and OFFICIALS
around her—

> BELLA REÁL
> We will rebuild... but not just
> our city. We must rebuild
> people's <u>faith</u>. In our
> institutions, in our elected
> officials, in <u>each other</u>. Together,
> we will learn to believe in
> Gotham again—

As **NIRVANA SWELLS**—

EXT. ABOVE GOTHAM SQUARE GARDEN—SUNRISE

The roof jammed with EVACUEES waiting to be air-lifted, as
FIRST RESPONDERS pull SURVIVORS through the skylight.

> BRUCE (VO)
> I'm starting to see now, I <u>have</u>
> had an effect here. But not the
> one I intended. Vengeance won't
> change the past... mine or
> anyone else's. I have to become
> <u>more</u>...

CLOSER: FIREMEN turn, struck by the sight of—**BATMAN,**
<u>caked in dried mud; he looks like hell—heads turn as he</u>
<u>carries AN INJURED WOMAN across the roof in his arms—</u>

                    BRUCE (VO)
People need hope. To <u>know</u>
someone's out there for them.
The city's angry. Scarred.
Like me...

As Batman puts her into a MED SLED, the woman CLUTCHES
him, distraught; Batman stiffens, unsure how to respond.

                    BRUCE (VO)
Our scars can destroy us... even
after the physical wounds have
healed. But if we survive them...

Batman leans in... returning the embrace... the sobbing
woman calms, releasing him... And the sled lifts...

                    BRUCE (VO)
They can transform us. They can
give us the power... to endure.
And the strength to fight.

HOLD ON BATMAN IN SILHOUETTE, watching the woman
ascend—

A HELICOPTER POV OVER HIM—AT THAT SAME MOMENT

A CHYRON APPEARS ON SCREEN: **"BATMAN VIGILANTE
SAVES THOUSANDS IN GOTHAM SQUARE"**—WE ARE
LOOKING AT A **TV** IN:

INT. ARKHAM PRISON FOR THE INSANE—SAME

THE TV sits in a GUARD STATION. Our view is a partially
obscured, sidelong perspective—we hear QUIET MOANING—

REVEAL **RIDDLER**—face smooshed to the security glass of his cell, craning to see the story in complete anguish...

> UNSEEN PRISONER'S VOICE
> Isn't that just terrible...? Him
> <u>raining on your parade</u> like that?
> What is it they say...? One day
> you're on top... the next, you're a
> <u>clown</u>. Well, let me tell you...
> there are <u>worse</u> things to be...

Riddler shrinks to the floor, totally despondent. Then:

> UNSEEN PRISONER'S VOICE
> Don't be <u>sad</u>... you did... <u>so well</u>...
> And you know, Gotham <u>loves</u> a
> comeback story...

Riddler rises, peering out of his cell, but can't see—

                         RIDDLER
                    ...who... who are you...?

                  UNSEEN PRISONER'S VOICE
                 Well that's the question isn't it?

                           (then)
                  Riddle me this... The less of them
                  you have... the more one is
                  worth.

Riddler ponders... then, finally... smiles hopefully...

                         RIDDLER
                      A friend...?

And the Unseen Prisoner begins to LAUGH... in the signature
JOKER style... the sound echoing us to—

EXT. RUN-DOWN GOTHAM CEMETERY—DUSK

Selina stands at a GRAVE: "MARIA KYLE". After a moment,
she turns, tears in her eyes, heading to her bike—her stray
cats poke their heads out of leather saddle bags—

                       A VOICE (OS)
                    ...you're leaving...

Selina turns, startled to see A FIGURE IN THE SHADOWS—
BATMAN, his motorcycle behind him. She's self-conscious.

                         SELINA
                  Jesus... don't you ever just say
                  hello?

He emerges, a sense of unfinished business between them.

> BATMAN
> —where will you go?

> SELINA
> I dunno, upstate...? Blüdhaven
> maybe...?

> (then, grins)
> Why... you asking me to <u>stay</u>?

But Batman says nothing. She darkens, worry in her voice:

> SELINA
> You know, this place is never
> gonna change. With Carmine
> gone, it's only gonna get <u>worse</u>
> for you—there's gonna be a real
> power grab—it'll be bloody—

> BATMAN
> I know, but the city <u>can</u> change—

> SELINA
> —it <u>won't</u>—!

> BATMAN
> —I have to <u>try</u>—

> SELINA
> —it's gonna <u>kill</u> you eventually,
> you <u>know</u> that...

SILENCE. Then, she tries to lighten things—a smile at an
impossible thought—

SELINA

...listen, why don't you come
with me? Get into some trouble.
We could knock off some CEOs.
Trust-fund types. It'll be fun.
The Bat and the Cat. Got a
nice ring...

—when she sees he's not looking at her; she follows his gaze to
the **BAT-SIGNAL** in the clouds—smiles, rueful—

SELINA

Who am I kidding? You're
already spoken for.

He looks back at her—she nods at the sky—

SELINA

You should go—

And then she turns, getting on her bike—when—

BATMAN

Selina...

She looks over—a pregnant silence as they stare—finally, he
speaks, resigned to letting her go—

BATMAN

Take care of yourself...

She nods a sad smile, starts her bike, heading off. Batman
watches her go, mounting his; he revs the engine, accelerating
after her—and for a moment, they chase through the

cemetery, echoes of their motorcycle scene early in the film... until, they split off opposite ways.

ON **BATMAN**, staring hard ahead... finally, HIS EYES MOVE TO HIS SIDE MIRROR, unable to resist one last look, **AS SHE RECEDES**... His eyes lift again, racing toward his city, a look of sheer determination—we HOLD, AS OUR VIEW ANGRILY VIBRATES WITH HIS EVER INCREASING SPEED... FASTER... AND **FASTER**... until, we...

CUT TO BLACK.

THE END

I N S I G H T
E D I T I O N S

PO Box 3088
San Rafael, CA 94912
www.insighteditions.com

f Find us on Facebook: www.facebook.com/InsightEditions
🐦 Follow us on Twitter: @insighteditions

ISBN: 978-1-64722-883-5

Publisher: Raoul Goff
VP of Licensing and Partnerships: Vanessa Lopez
VP of Creative: Chrissy Kwasnik
VP of Manufacturing: Alix Nicholaeff
VP, Editorial Director: Vicki Jaeger
Interior Design: *tabula rasa* graphic design
Case Design: Lola Villanueva
Editor: Rick Chillot
Editorial Assistant: Harrison Tunggal
Senior Production Editor: Katie Rokakis
Production Manager: Joshua Smith
Senior Production Manager, Subsidiary Rights: Lina s Palma Temena

ROOTS of PEACE REPLANTED PAPER

Insight Editions, in association with Roots of Peace, will plant two trees for each tree used in the manufacturing of this book. Roots of Peace is an internationally renowned humanitarian organization dedicated to eradicating land mines worldwide and converting war-torn lands into productive farms and wildlife habitats. Roots of Peace will plant two million fruit and nut trees in Afghanistan and provide farmers there with the skills and support necessary for sustainable land use.

Manufactured in China by Insight Editions

10 9 8 7 6 5 4 3 2 1